The emotional state of our culture today is one of hurt and heartache. With every retracted marriage vow, every breached contract, every unfulfilled political pledge, every "white lie"—in short, with every broken promise—lives are torn in two and hearts are trained to be distrustful. In *Unbroken Promises*, Mitchell Taylor breaks through this cynicism with a refreshing reminder of what true commitment looks like, the commitment of a faithful and trustworthy promise-keeping God. As Taylor shows in this book, true freedom and joy await those who choose to trust again.

—Bishop George Bloomer
Author of *Authority Abusers*
Pastor of Bethel Family Worship Center,
Durham, N.C.

I really believe that God will use this book mightily to bring about renewal in the hearts of His people. Mitch Taylor not only brings a message of hope for all who have been hurt by the broken promises of others, but he also issues a call to Christian men and women to be people of honor—trustworthy and always keeping their word. Taylor shares a special message that every Christian needs to hear.

—Hezekiah Walker
Author of *Destiny*
Gospel vocalist
Pastor of Love Fellowship Tabernacle,
Brooklyn, N.Y.

It's sad but true: We're more familiar with broken promises these days than we are with unbroken promises. A kept covenant is so rare that it catches us off guard—we don't know how to respond! Mitchell reminds us in his book that exactly the opposite should be true. He delves deep into the glories of God's promises and teaches those who have been wounded by broken promises how to trust once more.

—Liston Page, Jr.
Teacher, Preacher, and Evangelist
Pastor of Highway Church
Patterson, N.J.

UNBROKEN PROMISES

MITCHELL G. TAYLOR

W

WHITAKER
HOUSE

All Scripture quotations are taken from the King James Version (KJV) of the Bible.

UNBROKEN PROMISES

Center of Hope International
12-11 40th Avenue
Long Island City, NY, 11101
718-784-HOPE (office)
718-729-1288 (fax)
www.cohi.us

ISBN: 0-88368-871-9
Printed in the United States of America
© 2003 by Mitchell G. Taylor

Whitaker House
30 Hunt Valley Circle
New Kensington, PA 15068
web site: www.whitakerhouse.com

Library of Congress Cataloging-in-Publication Data

Taylor, Mitchell G., 1963–
  Unbroken promises / by Mitchell G. Taylor.
     p. cm.
  ISBN 0-88368-871-9 (trade paper : alk. paper)
  1. Christian life. 2. God—Promises. 3. Promises—Religious
aspects—Christianity. I. Title.
  BV4509.5 .T395 2003
  248.4—c21
                              2002154342

2 3 4 5 6 7 8 9 10 11 12 / 10 09 08 07 06 05 04 03

Table of Contents

Dedication

I dedicate this book to my mentor, teacher, and father,
Bishop Moses Taylor,
who is one of the greatest preachers in the world.

Introduction

Introduction

There was a point in time when the expression "I promise" could be taken seriously. Whenever a person said these words, he meant them. You could count on him carrying out whatever it was he promised to do.

I think you'll agree that those days are long gone. From the broken promises of politicians to the unkept promises of our closest friends, promises are seldom carried through anymore. Instead, "I promise" has become a catchphrase for pleasing others. No longer does "I promise" carry with it a sincere commitment to see an action through; it's merely an expression tacked on to words that we know others want to hear.

For instance, a politician might know his constituents want lower taxes, so he *promises* to cut taxes once he's elected, knowing very well all along that he might not be able to do so. Or perhaps a friend wants you to help him paint his house, so he *promises* to help you clean out your garage; a whole year later, your friend has yet to help you with your garage. Does this sound familiar?

Promises between people don't hold the value they once did. And when you've been burned once by a broken promise, it's hard to trust again. We build walls of doubt and quickly callous ourselves to accepting promises. "He doesn't mean that," we say. "He's just saying that to make me like him."

Fortunately, our God is not manipulative like mankind, nor does He break His promises.

> *God is not a man, that he should lie; neither the son of man, that he should repent: hath he said, and shall he not do it? or hath he spoken, and shall he not make it good?* (Numbers 23:19)

Unlike the promises of people, the promises of God are impossible to break. If He said it, it will come to pass!

Maybe you're having trouble believing this truth. Perhaps the Lord has spoken things into your life that have not yet been fulfilled. Take comfort in His Word, even during difficult times; know that He has not forgotten you. His Word is true, and He does not lie. He will see His promises through in His good and perfect time.

> *For the vision is yet for an appointed time, but at the end it shall speak, and not lie: though it tarry, wait for it; because it will surely come, it will not tarry.* (Habakkuk 2:3)

Please join me on this journey of discovering God's promises for His children. My prayer is that, as you realize how faithful your God is, you will begin not only to trust again but also to be more trustworthy yourself. May we come to understand and experience our Lord's unbroken promises, and may we mirror such faithfulness in our own lives as well!

—Mitchell G. Taylor

Chapter One

Sanctuary of Surrender: Where the Walls Come Down

Chapter 1

Sanctuary of Surrender: Where the Walls Come Down

W alk with me for a moment. We're in a sanctuary, a place of worship for the Lord God. All is still. And bright. It's so bright, in fact, that it takes your eyes a few moments to adjust. As you get used to the light, you start to see the many colors that comprise this brightness. Purples, reds, greens, and blues. Everywhere you turn, there are amazing splashes of vibrant light. You assume the colors come from the stained glass windows that most sanctuaries have. But as you direct your attention toward the windows, you find no windows. This kaleidoscope shines wholly on its own. Where are the windows? Even more importantly, where are the walls?

This is no traditional sanctuary. You're in a sanctuary without walls. The walls can't confine you here. If you call on the Lord to send life, life will come. The thirsty will drink water, the hungry will taste food, the naked will find clothing, and the homeless will be sheltered. Here, the Lord provides. Here, His promises are fulfilled.

In this church, miracles do happen. The wonderful works of the almighty God are shown, and He alone is glorified. Man-made boundaries don't get in the way here like they do in the natural church. Instead, walls of unbelief are banished; the confining fences of fear come down. All these barriers disappear until the glorious light of God's promises is all that's left.

In this church,
walls of unbelief are banished,
and the confining fences of fear
come down.

I don't want to be in a church where four walls of tradition control my destiny, where fear forever plagues me, and where faithlessness is my lot. I want to be in God's house, the place where bondage ends and limitless freedom begins, where a person can stagger through the doors in a drunken stupor and leave sobered and revived by God's mercy and love.

A Yielded Vessel

Before we can enter this sanctuary without walls, we need to become vessels without reservations—yielded vessels, that is, who are thirsty for whatever God has to put into us. We've got to be willing tabernacles, ready for the Holy Spirit to do His clearing out and cleaning up of our hearts. Only then can we enjoy this "sanctuary without walls" as the Holy Spirit expands the claustrophobic confinements that once restricted our lives.

When I first started preaching, God spoke to me about being a vessel like this. "I have yet to find a vessel that is totally yielded to Me," He said. "You can't imagine what I could do with a yielded vessel." He's continued to speak to me over the years about being yielded. Recently, God shared with me again. "If I had a vessel that could handle Me," He said, "you could see Me work."

Can you imagine being a vessel that God could fill? Can you picture being a clay pot that He would use? Whenever you walked into your workplace, people would see God. Whenever you opened your mouth to talk, people would hear Christ's words. Do you desire to be just such *"a vessel unto honour, sanctified, and meet for the master's use, and prepared unto every good work"* (2 Timothy 2:21)? Do you long to fully hold the treasures that He's designed for your clay pot? (See 2 Corinthians 4:7.)

I do. I want to know God's fullest. I want to taste in my life all that He has prepared for me. But before I do this, I have to do some preparing myself. With the Holy Spirit's help, I need to do "prep work" on my own heart so that I'm ready to receive God's fullness. God gave me three points about how I can prepare. I'd like to share these with you now.

Prepare for My Timing

First, God said, "Prepare for My timing." Remember, God is an eternal God. Peter talked about this in his second epistle: *"But, beloved, be not ignorant of this one thing, that one day is with the Lord as a thousand years, and a thousand years as one day"* (2 Peter 3:8). So, when it seems that God is taking too long to answer your prayers, don't forget that He's working from an eternal perspective. He has the big picture in mind, and the three days, four years, or five decades that you must wait for an answer are like nanoseconds in the scope of eternity. If we are to become fully yielded, uncomplaining vessels, we must understand this principle of God's timing; we must reorient our thinking to an eternal perspective; we must accept what often seem like unacceptably slow-coming answers.

Why does God take His time? If three days, four years, or five decades are all the same to Him, why doesn't He work in our lives right away? Why doesn't He tangibly answer our prayers as soon as we lift them up? Since we don't have His perfect eternal vision, we cannot fully know all His reasons; however, Scripture does provide us with a few principles for understanding the meaning of His method and the intention of His timing.

> When we serve the Lord, we need to make sure He gets all the glory and that everyone around us knows He's the true Star of the show.

For one thing, if God moved too quickly, we'd get out of the Spirit and into the flesh. If He answered all our prayers immediately and never required us to wait in patience and submission for His working, we'd start taking all the credit. "Look at me," we would say. "Look at this great thing I just did." When we're forced to wait in quietness and reliance on Him, however, we're less tempted to take credit. It's easier for us to remember that He gets the glory.

This holds an important lesson for our lives. When we serve the Lord, we need to make sure that He gets all the glory, all the praise, all the recognition, all the thanks. We should never step in and try to steal the applause. Instead, we should point everyone around us to the true Star of the show.

When I started writing this book, I prayed that God would be the focus of my effort. "God, if you use me, I'll tell the story," I prayed. "But I won't take the glory. You keep it

Lord; it belongs to You and to You alone." But I find that it's always a temptation to put myself at the center instead of God. C. S. Lewis discussed this in his book *The Problem of Pain.* He wrote:

> From the moment a creature becomes aware of God as God and of itself as self, the terrible alternative of choosing God or self for the centre is opened to it....We try, when we wake, to lay the new day at God's feet; before we have finished shaving, it becomes our day and God's share in it is felt as a tribute which we must pay out of "our own" pocket, a deduction from the time which ought, we feel, to be our own.*

It's a temptation for all of us to act like we're running the show. But, you see, some of us just cannot be blessed because we won't let God keep His glory. When God does something for or through you, don't take the glory. Please, don't take the credit; just tell the story. Say, "This is what happened, but to God goes *all* the glory!"

So, sometimes, God moves slowly to teach us reliance on Him, to train us how to give Him the glory. But He also moves slowly because, oftentimes, we're just not ready for His answer. He's ready to give the gift, but we're not ready to receive it. He's ready to fulfill His promises, but we're not ready to believe that He will fulfill them.

This is what happened to the children of Israel when God was about to lead them into the Promised Land. God had been faithful to His people: He had led them out of Egypt and out of Pharaoh's hand. He had guided them through the desert, through dryness and famine. He had taken them through the waters, through the Red Sea on top of dry ground. And yet, many Israelites still doubted God's

The Problem of Pain by C. S. Lewis, copyright © 1940, C. S. Lewis Pt. Ltd. Extract reprinted by permission. Excerpt taken from C. S. Lewis, *The Problem of Pain* (New York: HarperCollins, 2001), 70.

ability to bring them into the Promised Land. It was this unbelief, as the writer of Hebrews pointed out, that prevented the Israelites from receiving God's great promises; it was because of this unbelief that they wandered in the desert for so many years:

> But with whom was [God] grieved forty years? was it not with them that had sinned, whose carcases fell in the wilderness? and to whom sware he that they should not enter into his rest, but to them that believed not? so we see that they could not enter in because of unbelief. (Hebrews 3:17–19)

We should take note of the Israelites' bad example and avoid it ourselves. When God makes promises, He keeps them. Those promises are to be believed! Our God is not wishy-washy, changing His mind every few minutes. Whatever He says stands firm! If we doubt His promises, there's bound to be delay; but when we believe, then God pours forth all that He has promised in His perfect timing.

> There remaineth therefore a rest to the people of God. For he that is entered into his rest, he also hath ceased from his own works, as God did from his. Let us labour therefore to enter into that rest, lest any man fall after the same example of unbelief. (Hebrews 4:9–11)

Are you prepared for His timing? Believe on Him, give Him the glory, and prepare your life for His perfect pace.

Prepare for the Rigor

The second thing God told me was, "Prepare for the rigor." This might come as a surprise to some Christians since we often forget the hardships that come along with the Christian life. When we come to Christ, sometimes we mistakenly think that all is going to be easy and smooth. But the Scriptures are clear that quite the opposite is true. Like the calm before a storm or the quiet waters before a waterfall, periods of peacefulness in the Christian's life are usually followed by periods of trial. Consider these verses:

Beloved, think it not strange concerning the fiery trial which is to try you, as though some strange thing happened unto you: but rejoice, inasmuch as ye are partakers of Christ's sufferings; that, when his glory shall be revealed, ye may be glad also with exceeding joy.
(1 Peter 4:12–13)

My brethren, count it all joy when ye fall into divers temptations; knowing this, that the trying of your faith worketh patience. But let patience have her perfect work, that ye may be perfect and entire, wanting nothing.
(James 1:2–4)

Blessed are they which are persecuted for righteousness' sake: for theirs is the kingdom of heaven. Blessed are ye, when men shall revile you, and persecute you, and shall say all manner of evil against you falsely, for my sake. Rejoice, and be exceeding glad: for great is your reward in heaven: for so persecuted they the prophets which were before you. (Matthew 5:10–12)

And to him they agreed: and when they had called the apostles, and beaten them, they commanded that they should not speak in the name of Jesus, and let them go. And they departed from the presence of the council, rejoicing that they were counted worthy to suffer shame for his name. And daily in the temple, and in every house, they ceased not to teach and preach Jesus Christ. (Acts 5:40–42)

Therefore I endure all things for the elect's sakes, that they may also obtain the salvation which is in Christ Jesus with eternal glory. It is a faithful saying: For if we be dead with him, we shall also live with him: if we suffer, we shall also reign with him: if we deny him, he also will deny us. (2 Timothy 2:10–12)

Scripture assures us that life won't get easier once we've accepted Christ. Christians are not exempt from the struggles that all humans face. Disease, depression, bad days, and stubbed toes await the Christian, as well as the non-Christian. The fact is we're all living in a fallen world where hardship, hurt, and pain are always present. Until the Lord returns and builds His new heaven and new earth, heartache and tears are inevitable. (See Isaiah 65:17–19.) But we have a comfort as Christians since we are never left to face these struggles alone. The Lord has fashioned spiritual suits of armor for us and provided the Holy Spirit as our Comforter and Guide. (See Ephesians 6.) Were it not for His provision, we certainly could not handle life's hardships.

Disease, depression, bad days, and stubbed toes await the Christian, as well as the non-Christian, but we have a comfort as Christians since we are never left to face these struggles alone.

In addition to the difficulties that all humans must face, Christians face a certain set of struggles that are unique to them. In this sense, the Christian life is sometimes more rigorous than the non-Christian life! Do you think you can handle it? By yourself, you definitely can't. But if you're relying on the Lord, you can make it. He will provide you with the strength and endurance to finish the race marked out before you.

One of the most spiritually demanding and rigorous aspects of the Christian life is facing the Father Himself. Do you know what I'm talking about? I'm talking about looking at the Almighty and not falling over from fearful awe; I'm talking about being in His presence and handling all that glory; I'm talking about knowing how perfect He is and not crumbling under the realization of all your imperfections. That's what I'm talking about. Our God is a big God, an awesome God, a mighty God. Can you handle His rigor?

The Israelites learned this firsthand when they were in the desert. Before the Lord came, they spent a lot of time purifying and preparing their bodies for His presence. And when He did come, they trembled in fear, knowing that if they got too close, they would certainly die from seeing too much of His glory:

> And Moses came and called for the elders of the people, and laid before their faces all these words which the LORD commanded him. And all the people answered together, and said, All that the LORD hath spoken we will do. And Moses returned the words of the people unto the LORD. And the LORD said unto Moses, Lo, I come unto thee in a thick cloud, that the people may hear when I speak with thee, and believe thee for ever. And Moses told the words of the people unto the LORD. And the LORD said unto Moses, Go unto the people, and sanctify them to day and to morrow, and let them wash their clothes, and be ready against the third day: for the third day the LORD will come down in the sight of all the people upon mount Sinai. And thou shalt set bounds unto the people round about, saying, Take heed to yourselves, that ye go not up into the mount, or touch the border of it: whosoever toucheth the mount shall be surely put to death: there shall not an hand touch it, but he shall surely be stoned, or shot through; whether it be beast or man, it shall not live: when the trumpet soundeth long, they shall come up to the mount. And Moses went down from the mount unto the people, and sanctified the people; and they washed their clothes. And he said unto the people, Be ready against the third day: come not at your wives. And it came to pass on the third day in the morning, that there were thunders and

lightnings, and a thick cloud upon the mount, and the voice of the trumpet exceeding loud; so that all the people that was in the camp trembled. And Moses brought forth the people out of the camp to meet with God; and they stood at the nether part of the mount. And mount Sinai was altogether on a smoke, because the LORD descended upon it in fire: and the smoke thereof ascended as the smoke of a furnace, and the whole mount quaked greatly. And when the voice of the trumpet sounded long, and waxed louder and louder, Moses spake, and God answered him by a voice. And the LORD came down upon mount Sinai, on the top of the mount: and the LORD called Moses up to the top of the mount; and Moses went up. And the LORD said unto Moses, Go down, charge the people, lest they break through unto the LORD to gaze, and many of them perish. (Exodus 19:7–21)

Have you experienced rigor like this in your life? Have you been overwhelmed by the greatness of the Lord compared to the smallness of your own life? Moses experienced this in his personal life, too. As Exodus 33 records, he wasn't even allowed to see the Lord's face; he could look only at the Lord's back:

And [God] said, Thou canst not see my face: for there shall no man see me, and live. And the LORD said, Behold, there is a place by me, and thou shalt stand upon a rock: and it shall come to pass, while my glory passeth by, that I will put thee in a clift of the rock, and will cover thee with my hand while I pass by: and I will take away mine hand, and thou shalt see my back parts: but my face shall not be seen. (vv. 20–23)

Just like Aslan, the powerful yet gentle lion from C. S. Lewis' *Chronicles of Narnia* series, our God is always good, but He is not safe. He is far above us in His power, might, and holiness. Even though it is painful to realize how small and sinful we are compared to God's glory and perfection, we can have joy in the midst of this realization, for it is so beautiful that such a holy God would stoop to call us His children!

As Christians, we can experience pressure and rigor in our relationships, too. When the blessings of God are upon you and when His favor is evident your life, many people may not like you. These could be non-Christians who are intent on bringing you down, or even Christians who are jealous of or displeased with the way God is using you. They may not want to talk to you and might even devise mischief against you. Are you prepared for this rigor?

The Christian life isn't a cakewalk; it's very hard. But do you know what's so wonderful? Even all those tears, those pains, those pressures, and those heartaches are good! "Good?" you ask. "How on earth can they be good?!" Well, I'll tell you: because God uses them to refine you, to sort all the impurities out of your life so that you're ready to be more like Christ.

> *Wherein ye greatly rejoice, though now for a season, if need be, ye are in heaviness through manifold temptations: that the trial of your faith, being much more precious than of gold that perisheth, though it be tried with fire, might be found unto praise and honour and glory at the appearing of Jesus Christ.* (1 Peter 1:6–7)

If you're living the Christian life, stick with it. Remember what Jesus said: *"No man, having put his hand to the plow, and looking back, is fit for the kingdom of God"* (Luke 9:62). The Lord is committed to completing the good work He began in you; keep your hand on the plow so that He is able to finish that good work. (See Philippians 1:6.)

Prepare to Abide in Me

The third thing God revealed to me was, "Prepare to abide in Me." Jesus painted a picture of this in John 15 with His parable of the Vine and the Branches. Notice how many times He used the word *abide*:

I am the true vine, and my Father is the husband-man. Every branch in me that beareth not fruit he taketh away: and every branch that beareth fruit, he purgeth it, that it may bring forth more fruit. Now ye are clean through the word which I have spoken unto you. Abide in me, and I in you. As the branch cannot bear fruit of itself, except it abide in the vine; no more can ye, except ye abide in me. I am the vine, ye are the branches: He that abideth in me, and I in him, the same bringeth forth much fruit: for without me ye can do nothing. If a man abide not in me, he is cast forth as a branch, and is withered; and men gather them, and cast them into the fire, and they are burned. If ye abide in me, and my words abide in you, ye shall ask what ye will, and it shall be done unto you. Herein is my Father glorified, that ye bear much fruit; so shall ye be my disciples. As the Father hath loved me, so have I loved you: continue ye in my love. If ye keep my commandments, ye shall abide in my love; even as I have kept my Father's commandments, and abide in his love. (John 15:1–10)

The people to whom Jesus told this parable were familiar with agriculture and, therefore, understood the relationship between vines and branches. A branch is totally dependent upon the vine it comes from—for nutrients, for water, for life in general. If a branch does not remain connected to its vine, it dies. The same is true with Jesus and us. As this parable explains, Jesus is the True Vine. He is our Life Source, and if we are not connected to Him, we too will die; any dead, fruitless branches are thrown into the fire.

However, if we abide in Jesus, as branches abide in their vine, then Jesus will produce an abundance of fruit in our lives. And this is what pleases the Father. *"Herein is my Father glorified, that ye bear much fruit; so shall ye be my disciples"* (v. 8).

The word *abide* comes from the Greek word *meno*, which means "to stay in a given place, state, relation, or expectancy." It can also be translated "to continue," "to dwell," "to endure," "to be present," "to remain," "to stand," or "to tarry for." (See *Strong's Concordance*, #G3306). So, what about you? Are you *meno*-ing? Are you staying in the place God has assigned you? Are you continuing in the work He has given? Are you enduring the trial He has allowed? Are you tarrying for His presence? This is what it means to *meno*.

Are you *meno*-ing? Are you staying in the place God has assigned you? Are you continuing in the work He has given and enduring the trial He has allowed?

I'm sure you've heard of writer's block. It's a mind-set that writers sometimes fall into when they think they can't go any further. None of the words they're looking for seem easy to find, and writing becomes a major chore. Well, about midway through this chapter, writer's block set in on me. And, I'll tell you, I wanted to quit. I wanted to take a break and forget about writing this chapter—about writing this whole book, in fact! But then the Holy Spirit reminded me what this chapter was about: *abiding*. And He seemed to say, "You can't quit writing. This is where I want you to be right now. This is the task you are supposed to complete. *Meno*, My child, *meno*. Continue in this work, endure it, remain steadfast in it until the end."

God wants you to handle the rigor. Jesus said in verse four, *"Abide in me, and I in you. As the branch cannot bear fruit of itself, except it abide in the vine; no more can ye, except ye abide in me."* You can't move out of your place in the Vine. If He assigned you to be the sexton, then remain the sexton. If He assigned you to be the keyboardist, then be the keyboardist. If He assigned you to sing praise and worship, then keep on singing. But don't move out of your place in the Vine. You cannot bring forth fruit unless you stay connected to Him.

"If a man abide not in me, he is cast forth as a branch, and is withered; and men gather them, and cast them into the fire, and they are burned" (John 15:6). If you do leave the Vine, if you move out of your assigned place, the first thing the Father is going to do is cut you off, just like a dead branch. And then, since you are not connected to your life source, you will *"wither."*

A gentleman who had been with my ministry for several years left a while ago. He said that he had to leave because the Lord said it was time for him to go. I asked where He was going. "I don't know," he said, "but the Lord's going to show me." This floored me. "First of all," I told him, "the Lord would never tell you to leave a place that you're connected to, a place that is responsible for perpetuating your relationship with Him, without giving you some type of direction first. Why would He take you out of a place of growth to a place of fruitlessness?" The Lord will not ask us to leave our assigned places without giving us our new assignments first. We've got to stay connected, or else we will wither and fade away.

Verse six also says that the withered branches are *"burned."* What does this mean for us? I believe this symbolizes a loss of reward. The branch that does not *"meno"* is first *"cast forth,"* meaning it is disconnected from the vine. After this, it *"withers,"* meaning it fades away since it no longer has its life source. And, finally, the branch is *"burned,"* or separated, from the rewards it had when it was connected to the vine. The situation is similar in the spiritual life: Whenever we disconnect from our Vine, we no longer have claim to His spiritual treasures and promises. Those glorious gifts are for the branches that remain in Him. *Meno,* my friend, *meno.*

I'll admit: *Meno*-ing is not always easy. When things are going smoothly, no problem. If the right words are popping into my head and the pages are flying off the printer like crazy, for instance, I have no reservations about abiding, about continuing in the tasks at hand. But as soon as things get difficult—as soon as the writer's block sets in, or the non-Christians I meet start taunting me for my beliefs, or God's answers to prayer are coming too slowly—then *meno*-ing is tough. Praise God that He sends His Holy Spirit, our Comforter, to help us abide during these times.

Believe it or not, sometimes it's God Himself who makes abiding difficult. That sounds crazy, right? But it's true. As Jesus' parable of the Vine and the Branches illustrates, pruning is a big part of the Christian life. *"Every branch in me that beareth not fruit he taketh away: and every branch that beareth fruit, he purgeth it, that it may bring forth more fruit"* (v. 2). Even when we are abiding and are completely connected to the Vine, the Master Gardener trims back our branches, purging us so that we will be more fruitful. This is not an easy process; sometimes it hurts. But God intends it for good. Although pruning is painful, its result—an abundance of fruit—is immeasurably great.

Anybody can abide when it's a blessing to do so. But when the Lord decides to let you go through rigor, when your blessings come in the form of hardships, it is God's grace alone that enables you to abide, to remain and stay in the place He has chosen for your purging and growth. As King David said during a time of trial, *"I am in a great strait: let us fall now into the hand of the LORD; for his mercies are great: and let me not fall into the hand of man"* (2 Samuel 24:14). We can be confident when we are in the hands of our Lord, for He uses even the most painful experiences for His glory and our good.

Chapter Two

The Life of an Apple Tree

Chapter 2

The Life of an Apple Tree

Sitting on my kitchen table right now is a huge fruit bowl overflowing with shiny red apples from the grocery store. It is quite a sight. They're the kind of apples any kid would be proud to give to his schoolteacher. And they're tasty; I had one with my breakfast this morning and can't wait to have another one with lunch.

I never appreciated how much effort went into producing such fruit until recently, when I started taking note of the apple tree in our front yard. The tree is a nice size, fairly big, and it puts forth the most beautiful blossoms once springtime comes. But even though the tree is good-looking, its fruit is awful. The biggest apple I ever picked from it was barely bigger than a golf ball, and it was as mealy as an apple could be. The apples from my tree certainly do not compare to the grocery store apples sitting in my kitchen right now.

What's the difference between them? Why are the grocery store apples so wonderful while my apples are so bad?

I think you know the answer. It's because one batch of apples comes from an orchard where the trees are cared for day and night, while the other batch—my batch—comes from a tree that gets minimal human attention. The trees at the orchard are watered, trimmed, treated for pests, fed—all sorts of stuff! My tree doesn't get nearly as much attention.

You see, fruit doesn't just come forth; it has to be brought forth. There is a process that trees must go through to bear good fruit, and it is the same in your Christian life. Just as the orchard trees and my own apple tree had to withstand inclement weather, you too may have to endure some stress and strain in your life. And just as the orchard trees had to submit themselves to pruning and pesticide treatments, you too must submit to the wise care of God, your Gardener. You are God's tree, and He handles you with the hands of a gentle gardener. Even though the growth process may sometimes seem unbearable, your fruit will be worthy of His picking in the end.

Stages of Growth

As a fruit tree goes through many phases of growth in the natural world, so it is in the spirit realm with the saints of God. Let us now investigate eight stages for developing a mature, healthy apple tree and relate those stages to the process God takes us through in our growth process.

¤ Pruning:

In pruning, the tree is cut so that sunlight, essential for growth, can reach the inner branches. The Lord occasionally has to prune away needless branches in our lives that, otherwise, could prevent His light from shining upon our innermost parts. His light is as essential to our lives as sunlight is to any plant's life.

¤   Fertilization:

Before the fruit begins to grow in June, the tree is fertilized some time around April to ensure its capability for growth. *"And he answering said unto him, Lord, let it alone this year also, till I shall dig about it, and dung it"* (Luke 13:8). Even though being fertilized may seem like an unpleasant process to go through, it is necessary to provoke your growth and increase your stability.

Fruit doesn't just come forth;
it has to be brought forth.

¤   Grass Cutting:

Grass is grown in apple orchards to prevent the erosion of soil and to supplement organic composition. If the grass gets too long, however, it begins competing for moisture with the apple trees, so it must be cut four to six times each year.

Thou shalt not bow down thyself to them, nor serve them: for I the LORD thy God am a jealous God.
(Exodus 20:5)

Often there are things in our lives that compete with God, just as grass competes with an apple tree for nutrients. Since God is not willing that we should share His glory with any other, He sometimes must cut these things out of our lives. This ensures that He receives the glory He deserves, while also saving us from distractions that can rob us of necessary valuable nutrients.

¤ Pesticide:

To protect the apples from damage by insects and other pests, the apples must be sprayed with a safe pesticide. This helps prolong the tree's growing season, allowing the apples to reach full maturity. God too must sometimes come to kill the things within us that are preventing our growth, but the "pesticides" He uses will never damage the goods—us.

There hath no temptation taken you but such as is common to man: but God is faithful, who will not suffer you to be tempted above that ye are able; but will with the temptation also make a way to escape, that ye may be able to bear it.

(1 Corinthians 10:13)

God knows how to deliver you *"from the noisome pestilence"* (Psalm 91:3). He can destroy the enemy without destroying you in the process.

¤ Pollination:

Most apple trees must be cross-pollinated from a variety of apple trees in order to produce adequate fruit. Sometimes, as a means of cross-pollination, God moves us out of our comfort zones and places us around those who can stimulate our growth.

¤ Apple Thinning:

Each bud on an apple tree yields five flowers. In apple thinning, some of the flowers are removed while they're still in bloom to allow the remaining flowers to grow into larger, healthier apples. In the same way, God removes the unwanted (corrupt) or unnecessary (excess) fruit in our lives, which give only the illusion of success. The removal of these illusory fruits allows the good fruits to grow to the fullness of their potential.

¤   Foliage Removal and Apple Turning:

In foliage removal, the leaves that cast shadows on the apples, and thus prevent the sweetness of their pulp and the intense colors of their peels from fully developing, are removed. An experienced gardener must also turn the apples so that sunlight can hit them at all angles. (An inexperienced gardener will turn the fruit too far, causing it to fall to the ground). God, like a gardener, makes sure we get all the light we need.

The dayspring from on high hath visited us, to give light to them that sit in darkness and in the shadow of death, to guide our feet into the way of peace.
(Luke 1:78–79)

¤   Harvest:

After many months, the apples are finally picked, one by one and with care, so as not to damage them in the process. God uses those who understand our worth, value, and destiny to harvest us for the glory of His kingdom, so that our purpose might be fulfilled.

God is a gentle gardener. He will never cut off branches that we need or turn our apples so far that they fall off—unless they're bad apples that must be removed, that is. Yet, even though He is gentle, He still does His gardener duties, some of which are bound to be painful. But remember this important fact: It is all for His glory and for our good. We have to go through hard times of hurt before we can enjoy seasons of fruitfulness.

Hopefulness for Harvest Time

When a fruit tree goes through its fruit-bearing process, it endures a lot. In addition to all the pruning, fertilizing, pest treatments, and foliage removal, it deals with sun, snow, frost, and rain. It faces a lot of extremes.

I looked at the poor apple tree in front of my house one day. All winter long it looked so sad; eventually, I pronounced the tree dead. "Nothing good is coming from that tree this year," I concluded. "You're through now, brother." But when I arose one morning and peered through the window at the tree, I saw little buds on the limbs. That tree fought all winter. It struggled and struggled, and I thought it was going to die. I proclaimed its fate and its doom— "Yeah, you're gone brother"—and never thought to help it along. I never even wondered if it *might* survive. For me, it was a done deal: This tree was dead.

God is a gentle gardener. He will
never cut off branches
that we need.

But it wasn't. God had other plans. He held it in the warmth of His hands all winter long, keeping it alive and preparing it for harvest. He allowed the buds that had been lying dormant to burst forth in new life. He works this way in our lives, too. We all go through seasons of cold, seasons of winter, seasons of death. Other people may see you struggling through these blizzards and think that you haven't got a chance, just as I thought the apple tree was dead. "I think you're through," they conclude. "You're never going to bring forth anything good." But God works through these hard times, strengthening His trees for beautiful autumn harvests.

When we see our brothers and sisters in Christ struggling through life's storms and cold spells, let's not pronounce their deaths. Let's encourage them instead! Let's remind each other of the great Gardener, God, who reaps abundant harvests even after the worst of storms. Let's build each other up and tell each other, "Hang in there. Harvest time has almost come."

Chapter Three

Our God—
A God of Covenants

Chapter 3

Our God—A God of Covenants

What is commitment? What does it mean to be committed to somebody? Unfortunately, we don't have a very clear understanding of commitment in our society today. We do not grasp all that's required in pledging commitment to someone or something. Take marriage, for instance; marriage is supposed to be a sacred, rock-solid, unbreakable commitment between a man and a woman. In the United States, however, nearly half of all marriages end in divorce! Is this commitment? It's certainly not the kind of commitment God intended when He said, *"Therefore shall a man leave his father and his mother, and shall cleave unto his wife: and they shall be one flesh"* (Genesis 2:24).

But failure to understand commitment is not solely an American phenomenon. Nor is it confined to modern-day times. The question of how to live lives of commitment has troubled mankind throughout the world and for all ages. It's a human problem; our sinful desires continually vie for our attentions, pulling our efforts away from worthy commitments.

Our Lord, however, is a God of commitment and covenant, of solid pledges and unbroken promises. When He sees our lack of commitment to the things of heaven, it pains Him. He desires us to demonstrate commitment in our own lives, to mirror His promise-keeping character. To do this, we need to understand this element of His nature. Let's look closer at this quality of our covenant-making God.

The Lord Is Faithful

Have you ever noticed how often God's Word talks about His faithfulness? The Bible is very clear that our God is a God who both *makes* promises and *keeps* them:

> *Know therefore that the* LORD *thy God, he is God, the faithful God, which keepeth covenant and mercy with them that love him and keep his commandments to a thousand generations.* (Deuteronomy 7:9)

> *God is faithful, by whom ye were called unto the fellowship of his Son Jesus Christ our Lord.* (1 Corinthians 1:9)

> *There hath no temptation taken you but such as is common to man: but God is faithful, who will not suffer you to be tempted above that ye are able; but will with the temptation also make a way to escape, that ye may be able to bear it.* (1 Corinthians 10:13)

> *And the very God of peace sanctify you wholly; and I pray God your whole spirit and soul and body be preserved blameless unto the coming of our Lord Jesus Christ. Faithful is he that calleth you, who also will do it.* (1 Thessalonians 5:23–24)

> *But the Lord is faithful, who shall stablish you, and keep you from evil.* (2 Thessalonians 3:3)

> *If we confess our sins, he is faithful and just to forgive us our sins, and to cleanse us from all unrighteousness.* (1 John 1:9)

Whenever the Lord promises something, He sees that promise through. He is a promise maker. Even more importantly, He is a promise keeper. We can be sure that whatever He says will come to pass.

Whenever the Lord promises something, He sees that promise through.

This is what true commitment is all about: staying true to a promise, no matter what. How wonderful that we serve a God of promises! How wonderful that His track record for promise-keeping is perfect. He has never failed to carry out a promise. Our God is a God of promise and of covenant.

A *covenant* is a solemn vow or promise between two parties. Marriage, for instance, is a covenant; in it, a man and a woman vow to love each other until death parts them, no matter how good or how bad the circumstances may be. Even business contracts today are examples of covenants, for, in them, two parties agree to certain terms; if either party does not comply with those terms, consequences follow. Consequences always follow whenever a covenant is broken.

In Old Testament times, covenants were very common. God continually entered into covenants with His people, often sealing them with some symbolic image or action. In Genesis, for instance, God sent a rainbow to Noah, sealing His promise to never again flood the earth.

And I will establish my covenant with you; neither shall all flesh be cut off any more by the waters of a flood; neither shall there any more be a flood to destroy the earth. And God said, This is the token of the covenant which I make between me and you and every living creature that is with you, for perpetual generations: I do set my bow in the cloud, and it shall be for a token of a covenant between me and the earth. And it shall come to pass, when I bring a cloud over the earth, that the bow shall be seen in the cloud: and I will remember my covenant, which is between me and you and every living creature of all flesh; and the waters shall no more become a flood to destroy all flesh. (Genesis 9:11–15)

God entered into another covenant a little later in Genesis. In this one, God promised Abraham that He would increase his seed so that all mankind would descend from him. God sealed this promise with a special sacrificial ceremony, which demonstrated how devoted He was to keeping His word:

And [Abraham] *took unto him all these, and divided them in the midst, and laid each piece one against another: but the birds divided he not. And when the fowls came down upon the carcases, Abram drove them away. And when the sun was going down, a deep sleep fell upon Abram; and, lo, an horror of great darkness fell upon him. And* [God] *said unto Abram, Know of a surety that thy seed shall be a stranger in a land that is not theirs, and shall serve them; and they shall afflict them four hundred years; and also that nation, whom they shall serve, will I judge: and afterward shall they come out with great substance. And thou shalt go to thy fathers in peace; thou shalt be buried in a good old age. But in the fourth genera-tion they shall come hither again: for the iniquity of the Amorites is not yet full. And it came to pass, that, when the sun went down, and it was dark, behold a smok-ing furnace, and a burning lamp that passed between those pieces. In the same day the* LORD *made a cov-enant with Abram, saying, Unto thy seed have I given this land, from the river of Egypt unto the great river, the river Euphrates.* (Genesis 15:10–18)

God used covenants throughout the Bible. The following passage from Joshua sums up the fulfillment of just a few of those covenants:

And Joshua gathered all the tribes of Israel to Shechem, and called for the elders of Israel, and for their heads, and for their judges, and for their officers; and they presented themselves before God. And Joshua said unto all the people, Thus saith the LORD God of Israel, Your fathers dwelt on the other side of the flood in old time, even Terah, the father of Abraham, and the father of Nachor: and they served other gods. And I took your father Abraham from the other side of the flood, and led him throughout all the land of Canaan, and multiplied his seed, and gave him Isaac. And I gave unto Isaac Jacob and Esau: and I gave unto Esau mount Seir, to possess it; but Jacob and his children went down into Egypt. I sent Moses also and Aaron, and I plagued Egypt, according to that which I did among them: and afterward I brought you out. And I brought your fathers out of Egypt: and ye came unto the sea; and the Egyptians pursued after your fathers with chariots and horsemen unto the Red sea. And when they cried unto the LORD, he put darkness between you and the Egyptians, and brought the sea upon them, and covered them; and your eyes have seen what I have done in Egypt: and ye dwelt in the wilderness a long season. And I brought you into the land of the Amorites, which dwelt on the other side Jordan; and they fought with you: and I gave them into your hand, that ye might possess their land; and I destroyed them from before you. Then Balak the son of Zippor, king of Moab, arose and warred against Israel, and sent and called Balaam the son of Beor to curse you: but I would not hearken unto Balaam; therefore he blessed you still: so I delivered you out of his hand. And ye went over Jordan, and came unto Jericho: and the men of Jericho fought against you, the

Amorites, and the Perizzites, and the Canaanites, and the Hittites, and the Girgashites, the Hivites, and the Jebusites; and I delivered them into your hand. And I sent the hornet before you, which drave them out from before you, even the two kings of the Amorites; but not with thy sword, nor with thy bow. And I have given you a land for which ye did not labour, and cities which ye built not, and ye dwell in them; of the vineyards and oliveyards which ye planted not do ye eat. (Joshua 24:1–13)

The Bible leaves no room for doubt that our God is a covenant-making God who always keeps His promises.

Who Are These Covenants For?

So far, most of the covenants we've been discussing were directed toward Israel, God's chosen people of the Old Testament. We are Gentiles, however, meaning we are not Jewish. We are not, in the traditional sense, "God's chosen people." Do these covenants apply to us or not?

A passage in Matthew may seem to suggest that God's covenants do not apply to Gentiles. Here, Jesus spoke to His disciples, all of whom were of the Jewish tradition.

Therefore I say unto you, Take no thought for your life, what ye shall eat, or what ye shall drink; nor yet for your body, what ye shall put on. Is not the life more than meat, and the body than raiment? Behold the fowls of the air: for they sow not, neither do they reap, nor gather into barns; yet your heavenly Father feedeth them. Are ye not much better than they? Which of you by taking thought can add one cubit unto his stature? And why take ye thought for raiment? Consider the lilies of the field, how they grow; they toil not, neither do they spin: and yet I say unto you, That even Solomon in all his glory was not arrayed like one of these. Wherefore, if God so clothe

*the grass of the field, which to day is, and to morrow
is cast into the oven, shall he not much more clothe
you, O ye of little faith? Therefore take no thought,
saying, What shall we eat? or, What shall we drink?
or, Wherewithal shall we be clothed? (For after all
these things do the Gentiles seek:) for your heavenly
Father knoweth that ye have need of all these things.*
(Matthew 6:25–32)

Jesus was speaking to Jews here, to those who were in
covenant with Him. He came to the Jews first; He came to
His own. "You're joined to Me by covenant," He basically told
them. "Since you are joined with Me, you have no reason
to worry about your needs being met. When you are in covenant with Me, whatever you need I'll supply." When He said
to His disciples, in effect, "You're talking like the Gentiles,"
He was rebuking them because the Gentiles were not in covenant with God at that time. He was calling them to remember their covenant status as Jews, God's chosen people.

Does this mean that we, as Christian Gentiles, do not
have covenant status? Not at all! For, with Christ's life, death,
and resurrection, the covenant was opened up to people of
all races and nations.

*And they of the circumcision which believed were
astonished, as many as came with Peter, because
that on the Gentiles also was poured out the gift of the
Holy Ghost.* (Acts 10:45)

*And the apostles and brethren that were in Judaea
heard that the Gentiles had also received the word of
God.* (Acts 11:1)

*Then Paul and Barnabas waxed bold, and said, It was
necessary that the word of God should first have been
spoken to you: but seeing ye put it from you, and judge
yourselves unworthy of everlasting life, lo, we turn to
the Gentiles. For so hath the Lord commanded us,*

saying, I have set thee to be a light of the Gentiles, that thou shouldest be for salvation unto the ends of the earth. And when the Gentiles heard this, they were glad, and glorified the word of the Lord: and as many as were ordained to eternal life believed.
(Acts 13:46–48)

Now I say that Jesus Christ was a minister of the circumcision for the truth of God, to confirm the promises made unto the fathers: and that the Gentiles might glorify God for his mercy; as it is written, For this cause I will confess to thee among the Gentiles, and sing unto thy name. And again he saith, Rejoice, ye Gentiles, with his people. And again, Praise the Lord, all ye Gentiles; and laud him, all ye people. And again, Esaias saith, There shall be a root of Jesse, and he that shall rise to reign over the Gentiles; in him shall the Gentiles trust. Now the God of hope fill you with all joy and peace in believing, that ye may abound in hope, through the power of the Holy Ghost. And I myself also am persuaded of you, my brethren, that ye also are full of goodness, filled with all knowledge, able also to admonish one another. Nevertheless, brethren, I have written the more boldly unto you in some sort, as putting you in mind, because of the grace that is given to me of God, that I should be the minister of Jesus Christ to the Gentiles, ministering the gospel of God, that the offering up of the Gentiles might be acceptable, being sanctified by the Holy Ghost. (Romans 15:8–16)

And if ye be Christ's, then are ye Abraham's seed, and heirs according to the promise.
(Galatians 3:29)

And have put on the new man, which is renewed in knowledge after the image of him that created him: where there is neither Greek nor Jew, circumcision nor uncircumcision, Barbarian, Scythian, bond nor free: but Christ is all, and in all.

(Colossians 3:10–11)

With Christ's coming, the promise of salvation extended to the Gentiles. The Jews were no longer God's only "chosen people." We, as Gentiles, were adopted. We were grafted into the covenant. With Christ's coming, Gentiles could belong to God, too, just as the Jews did.

You have a contract with God.
He will take care of you.

You have a contract with God. He will take care of you, just as He took care of Israel during its forty years of wandering in the desert. Before you learned your own name, before you were formed in your mother's womb, even before your parents met, God knew you. He knew you intimately, just as He does now, inside and out. When the Lord talks about knowing you, He's not talking about casual contact. He's talking about an unmatchable intimacy that He's committed to sustaining. He is in covenant with those He's chosen, and the Lord God never backs out of a covenant. He is committed to fulfilling His promises.

The King's Kingdom

But seek ye first the kingdom of God, and his righteousness; and all these things shall be added unto you. (Matthew 6:33)

If you want to stay in covenant with the Lord, you need to seek Him. You cannot maintain the contract value if you're avoiding the King. You must dwell where He dwells—in the King's kingdom.

This, seeking His dwelling place, is how we stay in covenant with the King. If I could just hang out where the King hangs out, surely I would be blessed. I might not get everything He has, but staying there long enough and feasting on the crumbs that fall from His table would be enough to satisfy my needs.

Are you seeking the kingdom? Do you daily talk to the King and read His "letter" to you? Is your time spent with other kingdom dwellers, or only with those who don't know the King? Seek first His kingdom. This is the way to stay in covenant.

The Godparent Versus God

As we've seen, our God is a God of promises. He has made covenants throughout history, and He never breaks a single one. He is a promise-making and promise-keeping God—and He desires us to be faithful in promise-keeping as well. *"For I have given you an example, that ye should do as I have done to you"* (John 13:15).

How do we match up? Can we keep our promises just as God keeps His? How faithful are we? Well, the truth of the matter is that our ability to make and keep promises pales next to God's. Even the most earnest and eager of Christians falls short. God is faithful; we continually fight faithlessness. He is steadfast; we lose our steadiness fast. He is constantly committed; we constantly commit the sin of promise-breaking.

For example, consider the task of being a godparent. This is a decision that takes commitment. When you become a godparent, you become committed to the care of a child. You don't want to be the godparent just because the baby is cute or because the mother is your best friend; you pledge, or commit, to stand alongside the parents and raise the child in fear and admonition of the Lord because you desire to serve the Lord through serving this family.

But no matter how earnest your commitment is, you are bound to fall short. There will be times when you set bad examples for the child, as well as times when you cannot lend a listening ear. Why? Because you are human. Mankind is sinful, and no matter how good our intentions are, we will inevitably mess up.

When the Lord talks about knowing you, He's not talking about casual contact. He's talking about unmatchable intimacy.

God is not like this. Instead He is perfect and unchanging. When He commits to being our Father, we can take that commitment to the bank. He never falls short and never lets us down. His commitment is perfect commitment. *"He which hath begun a good work in you will perform it until the day of Jesus Christ"* (Philippians 1:6). Any work that God begins, He finishes.

If God's commitment is so perfect and ours is so imperfect, should we even *try* to learn commitment? Is it just an uphill battle that we never will win?

It's very easy to fall into thinking like this, but we shouldn't. God has called us to follow after the example of His Son in all that we do.

> *For what glory is it, if, when ye be buffeted for your faults, ye shall take it patiently? but if, when ye do well, and suffer for it, ye take it patiently, this is acceptable with God. For even hereunto were ye called: because Christ also suffered for us, leaving us an example, that ye should follow his steps.* (1 Peter 2:20–21)

Yes, it's true that our level of commitment will always pale next to God's. But it's also true that we should strive to follow His example, for this pleases Him. Just as you want God to commit to the many blessings outlined throughout His sixty-six books of wisdom and understanding, God wants you to exhibit relentless commitment and praise. He has provided the ultimate example of what it means to be committed. Let us praise Him for His commitment to us, and let us imitate such commitment in our own lives.

Chapter Four

Releasing the Wealth to Gain God's Finest

Chapter 4

Releasing the Wealth to Gain God's Finest

And, behold, one came and said unto him, Good Master, what good thing shall I do, that I may have eternal life? And he said unto him, Why callest thou me good? there is none good but one, that is, God: but if thou wilt enter into life, keep the commandments. He saith unto him, Which? Jesus said, Thou shalt do no murder, Thou shalt not commit adultery, Thou shalt not steal, Thou shalt not bear false witness, Honour thy father and thy mother: and, Thou shalt love thy neighbour as thyself. The young man saith unto him, All these things have I kept from my youth up: what lack I yet? Jesus said unto him, If thou wilt be perfect, go and sell that thou hast, and give to the poor, and thou shalt have treasure in heaven: and come and follow me. But when the young man heard that saying, he went away sorrowful: for he had great possessions.

—Matthew 19:16–22

What *"great possessions"* in your life are keeping you from Christ? Are things of this world distracting you from that which is eternal? For the rich man, it was his wealth. Everything else in his life was fine, for he kept the commandments perfectly. But this one thing, his wealth, was his downfall. He could not bring himself to let go of his wealth so that he could taste eternal life to its fullest.

Do you have wealth in your life that you're not willing to let go of? Remember, "wealth" includes more than stocks and bonds, gold and silver, or cash and credit cards. Wealth is anything that takes center stage in your life. Wealth is what you value. Wealth is whatever your heart treasures most. *"For where your treasure is, there will your heart be also"* (Matthew 6:21).

If God asked you to release your wealth and follow Him, just as Christ asked the rich man to give his riches to the poor, would you do it? Would you let go of your earthly treasures to gain God's finest? How much would you forfeit for the kingdom?

> *Lay not up for yourselves treasures upon earth, where moth and rust doth corrupt, and where thieves break through and steal: but lay up for yourselves treasures in heaven, where neither moth nor rust doth corrupt, and where thieves do not break through nor steal.*
> (vv. 19–20)

When challenged on matters of the heart such as this, many people reason that they don't need to take action. "I would give up my wealth in a second," they say, "but God knows my heart. He knows that He's the most important thing in my life. I don't need to prove it." When we think this way, though, it's very easy to let other things slip into primary position without even realizing it. If God is number one, however, we should be able to take actions that show it.

What doth it profit, my brethren, though a man say he hath faith, and have not works? can faith save him?...Even so faith, if it hath not works, is dead, being alone. Yea, a man may say, Thou hast faith, and I have works: show me thy faith without thy works, and I will show thee my faith by my works. Thou believest that there is one God; thou doest well: the devils also believe, and tremble. But wilt thou know, O vain man, that faith without works is dead?...For as the body without the spirit is dead, so faith without works is dead also. (James 2:14, 17–20, 26)

What is closest to your heart? Are you willing to let go of it to receive God's finest?

Do Not Disturb

When the disciples studied Christ's interaction with the rich man, it troubled their spirits. They began to realize that they had to operate under an umbrella of faith, and that Jesus was not concerned with the same things that concerned them.

Then said Jesus unto his disciples, Verily I say unto you, That a rich man shall hardly enter into the kingdom of heaven. And again I say unto you, It is easier for a camel to go through the eye of a needle, than for a rich man to enter into the kingdom of God. When his disciples heard it, they were exceedingly amazed, saying, Who then can be saved? But Jesus beheld them, and said unto them, With men this is impossible; but with God all things are possible. (Matthew 19:23–26)

The disciples' concerns were with resources, accommodations, and sticking to the budget. However, Jesus had something else in mind; His concern was with the soul of a person. The disciples began to realize the importance of salvation for the soul. They began to understand that salvation does not rely on earthly possessions; instead, a person desiring salvation needs to put God first in His life, above abundance and wealth.

Problems arise in our lives when we want to be religious but not completely sold out to God. Sometimes, we want God to control certain areas of our lives. On matters close to our hearts, however, we post "Do Not Disturb" signs, forbidding the Lord to enter. This is pure defiance. Our unwillingness to surrender these secret corners of our lives dilutes our professed commitment to God and His Word.

Confronting Reality— Slave to Sin, Freed in Christ

Why do we post these "Do Not Disturb" signs? Oftentimes, it's because we fear God will place restrictions on our lives. *"If ye love me, keep my commandments"* (John 14:15). We worry that God's commandments will limit our lives. We fret about the spiritual boundaries and borders that we know He'll soon put up.

> If God is number one, you should be able to take actions that show it.

While we worry about what we call restrictions, the reality is that full freedom comes only from the Lord. *"If the Son therefore shall make you free, ye shall be free indeed"* (John 8:36). The devil deceives us into thinking salvation is a list of laws and legalities, a bunch of *dos* and *don'ts*. People avoid this because it restricts them. It takes them out of their zone of pleasure, their place of comfort, and their natural environment—sin.

Do you doubt that sin is your natural environment? It really is. Think through this with me for a second: No one had to teach you how to do wrong as a child. You knew how to get into trouble from the start; it was inherently in you. This is because every person is born a slave to sin. Not only do we sin, we can't even *not* sin. No matter how hard we try by ourselves, we cannot avoid sinning, for we are sinful beings. Until we accept Christ's gift of salvation, we are bound to sin.

> *Behold, I was shapen in iniquity, and in sin did my mother conceive me.*   (Psalm 51:5)

> *Know ye not, that to whom ye yield yourselves servants to obey, his servants ye are to whom ye obey; whether of sin unto death, or of obedience unto righteousness?*   (Romans 6:16)

> *If we say that we have no sin, we deceive ourselves, and the truth is not in us. If we confess our sins, he is faithful and just to forgive us our sins, and to cleanse us from all unrighteousness. If we say that we have not sinned, we make him a liar, and his word is not in us.*
> (1 John 1:8–10)

As these verses show, bondage—not freedom—is found in the life of sin. While we may fear that the Christian life will impose all kinds of restrictions, this is far from the truth. A life in Christ actually *frees* us from sin's bondage, while opening up to us pathways of life, possibility, and potential.

> *But God be thanked, that ye were the servants of sin, but ye have obeyed from the heart that form of doctrine which was delivered you. Being then made free from sin, ye became the servants of righteousness. I speak after the manner of men because of the infirmity of your flesh: for as ye have yielded your members servants to uncleanness and to iniquity unto iniquity; even so now yield your members servants to righteousness unto holiness. For when ye were the servants of sin, ye were free from righteousness. What fruit had ye then in those things whereof ye are now ashamed? for the end of those things is death. But now being made*

free from sin, and become servants to God, ye have your fruit unto holiness, and the end everlasting life. For the wages of sin is death; but the gift of God is eternal life through Jesus Christ our Lord.
(Romans 6:17–23)

Are you posting "Do Not Disturb" signs on your heart? Are you refusing to surrender the steering wheel of your life to the Savior? If you are, you're choosing the road marked DANGER, for the path to life is found only in Christ. Remember, the life of sin is the life of bondage; the life in Christ is the life of freedom.

On matters close to our hearts, we often post "Do Not Disturb" signs, forbidding the Lord to enter.

The Bible declares that, if you have accepted Christ as your Savior, your body is the temple of God.

What? know ye not that your body is the temple of the Holy Ghost which is in you, which ye have of God, and ye are not your own? For ye are bought with a price: therefore glorify God in your body, and in your spirit, which are God's. (1 Corinthians 6:19–20)

Are you living as a temple for the Lord? You don't belong to yourself; you have been bought with a price. Your life must reflect the Lord who lives in you. Some of us, before we came into relationship with God, had relationships with drugs, drinking, and other things that controlled our minds and bodies. The cravings of our physical bodies engulfed our minds, and, instead of enjoying lives of peace, we struggled with a continual warring within.

Maybe, even as a Christian, you still struggle with this. Instead of facing reality, you turn to drugs or alcohol as an escape. Trying to fill the void in your life with temporal pleasures such as these will only prolong your misery. Christ alone can fill the emptiness in your life. It has been said that the seventeenth century philosopher Blaise Pascal expressed it this way: "There is a God-shaped vacuum in the heart of every man which cannot be filled by any created thing, but only by God, the Creator, made known through Jesus Christ." In other words, each of us has a spiritual hole that's hungry for the Lord. And nothing can satisfy that hungry spot except the Lord Himself.

I've heard it said that celery is a good food for weight loss; it barely has any calories, and the calories it does have are burned off by chewing it. This food would not be good for a person who's genuinely hungry and needs to get some energy into his system. That person would just keep eating, and eating, and eating the celery without getting one ounce of strength from it!

Trying to fill our "God-shaped vacuum" with anything other than God is sort of like trying to fill up an empty stomach with celery. We can try to fill our spiritual void with sex, drugs, money, power, good looks, alcohol, expensive cars, and material goods, but none of these things will fill our God-shaped hole. If anything, these things will only make the hole bigger— just as celery can never fill a person up with calories.

The old church father St. Augustine explained this wonderfully in his *Confessions*: "For You made us for Yourself, and our hearts are restless until they rest in You."* Until we know Jesus Christ as Lord and Savior, our hearts will be hungry and restless. We will only find satisfaction and rest in our Lord Jesus Christ.

Confronting reality allows you to stop hiding from life; it frees you to boldly face the fears before you. If you have "Do Not Disturb" signs tacked up, you're not going to be happy;

---

* St. Augustine, *Confessions*, (New Kensington: Whitaker House, 1996), Book I, p. 11.

you're going to feel trapped, miserable, and enslaved to sinful desires. But once you take down those signs and invite Christ in, joy and freedom await you!

Christ came so that you might have life. *"The thief cometh not, but for to steal, and to kill, and to destroy: I am come that they might have life, and that they might have it more abundantly"* (John 10:10). If He came so that you might have life, that means you were already dead before He came. *"Sin, when it is finished, bringeth forth death"* (James 1:15). You're not here to be bound; you're here to be free and to walk in the abundance of life. Take down those "Do Not Disturb" signs. Let the Lord have full reign over your life. Only then will you truly experience life.

Giving God the Best—
Using Your Natural Gifts in Your New Life

If you think that just because you're in the church you're supposed to put on a sad face and act downtrodden, you're sorely mistaken. It is not God's will for you to go around looking like you've lost everything. Salvation is not synonymous with poverty; instead, it signifies new life, new beginnings, and a new spirit!

I'm very concerned for people who claim to have a relationship with Christ yet lack the evidence in their lives. If you're a child of God, you should display evidence of that relationship. People should be able to look at you and see Him in your life.

Early in her career, the Christian artist Amy Grant had a song about this called *Father's Eyes*. Do you have your Father's eyes? Or do people see only *your eyes* when they look at your life? Don't be content with being just you. Seek out opportunities for spiritual growth, every day, so that your life will come to reflect your heavenly Father.

I am crucified with Christ: nevertheless I live; yet not I, but Christ liveth in me: and the life which I now live in the flesh I live by the faith of the Son of God, who loved me, and gave himself for me. (Galatians 2:20)

If we could only grasp the true meaning of this text from Galatians and then demonstrate it in our lives, we would see God manifested like never before. You see, it's not me who lives. As Paul explains here in Galatians, my old sinful self is dead; it was crucified with Christ when I repented of my sins and asked Jesus to be my Savior. The spiritual life that is in me now is wholly from Christ, who rose from the dead and let me rise with Him. I have a new life.

Trying to fill our "God-shaped vacuum" with anything other than God is sort of like trying to fill up an empty stomach with celery.

We need to remember our new status in Christ whenever we are tempted to fall into the sins of our "old nature." Unfortunately, temptations like this are inevitable. Paul wrote about this in Romans when he discussed the ongoing battle between his old sinful desires and his new spirit-led longings.

If then I do that which I would not, I consent unto the law that it is good. Now then it is no more I that do it, but sin that dwelleth in me. For I know that in me (that is, in my flesh,) dwelleth no good thing: for to will is present with me; but how to perform that which is good I find not. For the good that I would I do not: but the evil which I would not, that I do. Now if I do that I would not, it is no more I that do it, but sin that dwelleth in me. I find then a law, that, when I would do good, evil is present with me. For I delight in the law of God after the inward

man: but I see another law in my members, warring against the law of my mind, and bringing me into captivity to the law of sin which is in my members.
(Romans 7:16–23)

Even after you become a Christian, you will still want to do sinful things; until Christ returns, there will always be this spiritual battle within each Christian. During these times of struggle between the old self and the new self, it's helpful to remember your new-self status in Christ; remembering this makes maintaining victory possible.

We can't go to the next level unless we're willing to give God all that He requires, even if that means giving up our most cherished temporal pleasures. Moses understood this, for he chose *"rather to suffer affliction with the people of God, than to enjoy the pleasures of sin for a season"* (Hebrews 11:25).

This verse reminds us that sin can be pleasurable—but only for a season. This pleasure is not only short-lived, but also costly, for sin always separates us from God. Once we realize the superiority of a relationship with Christ, we will be eager to abandon sin.

But what things were gain to me, those I counted loss for Christ. Yea doubtless, and I count all things but loss for the excellency of the knowledge of Christ Jesus my Lord: for whom I have suffered the loss of all things, and do count them but dung, that I may win Christ.　　　　　(Philippians 3:7–8)

Once you become a Christian, you have a new life. You are a completely new creation, and your life should reflect that fact: *"Therefore if any man be in Christ, he is a new creature: old things are passed away; behold, all things are become new"* (2 Corinthians 5:17). But when you become a new creation, this doesn't mean God changes your character or your personality, your gifts or your talents. He maintains the uniqueness of you and preserves the person He carefully knit together in your mother's womb. Did you like music before you were saved? You'll probably still like it afterwards. Have you always had a special gift for fixing things—cars, broken radios, whatever—even before you became a Christian? These things were manifested in your life. Why? Because He knit these things into your being during your creation. He's not about to abolish all the good things He placed in you at your first birth, your physical birth.

> *For thou hast possessed my reins: thou hast covered me in my mother's womb. I will praise thee; for I am fearfully and wonderfully made: marvellous are thy works; and that my soul knoweth right well. My substance was not hid from thee, when I was made in secret, and curiously wrought in the lowest parts of the earth. Thine eyes did see my substance, yet being unperfect; and in thy book all my members were written, which in continuance were fashioned, when as yet there was none of them.* (Psalm 139:13–16)

I remember partying before I was saved; nobody could party like I could. This reflected a big part of my character: Everything I do, I do it to the extreme. Now that I'm saved, I use this personality trait for God's glory. Everything that I do now is still to the extreme—but it's for God, not for me. Since the Lord has blessed me with a spirit of excellence, I can't do anything halfway. I must always give my best. The big difference between now and my party days is *whom* the excellence is for. I used to party hard for my own enjoyment; now I work hard for God's glory.

God has used my organizational skills in much the same way. When I was in the world, I wanted everything done just right. I was called "the organizer" because I was so meticulous about organizing things. Although I was the smallest on the streets for my age, I was always surrounded by really strong people. They knew that I was able to keep our ill-gotten money organized and flowing smoothly. If I was able to do this in a worldly setting, why shouldn't I use these same organizational skills in the church?

Sin can be pleasurable—but only for a season.

Many of us talk about our creativity and accomplishments before we knew Christ. If we exercised our gifts so freely in the world, then why do we lose all enthusiasm just because we're in the church? Don't come into the body of Christ and become witless. If you had good gifts that you used for the world, you need to sharpen those gifts for the kingdom. God has blessed you with many natural gifts. Use them for His kingdom, for this pleases the King.

All or Nothing

We can't serve God with only half-baked religion, willing to give Him our confession but not our complete surrender; He deserves all of us. Oftentimes, we ration out to God what we feel He should have while withholding the parts of our lives that we think we need to hold on to.

But if you could only see what God is ready to give you in place of those things you refuse to release, you would let go of them in a second. If you could understand fully that His gifts are like gold while everything else is like garbage, you would not hold on to the things of this world so tightly. You'd be willing to let go of it all—the earthly possessions, the pride, the prestige, the positions of power—just so you could taste a drop of His goodness and grace.

Can you imagine if God had a yielded vessel—somebody who submitted to His will and never took God's glory for himself? As God's Word reminds us, everything here is His to begin with. If we pretend that we're in charge or that we're the ones ruling our lives, we only deceive ourselves. *"For every beast of the forest is mine, and the cattle upon a thousand hills"* (Psalm 50:10). It all belongs to God. *"The earth is the LORD's, and the fulness thereof; the world, and they that dwell therein"* (Psalm 24:1). Our God is a sovereign God. The sooner we acknowledge this, the better, for the greatest joy comes to those who cherish the Lord's commands.

> *And I will delight myself in thy commandments, which I have loved. My hands also will I lift up unto thy commandments, which I have loved; and I will meditate in thy statutes.* (Psalm 119:47–48)

The rich man from Matthew 19 reminds me of many churchgoers today who stand at the door of deliverance but never enter because they won't surrender all of their lives. Their answer lies within reach; they're entangled in it yet unable to reap its benefits because they don't grasp the concept of "all or nothing."

> *I know thy works, that thou art neither cold nor hot: I would thou wert cold or hot. So then because thou art lukewarm, and neither cold nor hot, I will spue thee out of my mouth.* (Revelation 3:15–16)

We cannot compromise spirituality for the sake of carnal satisfaction; if our lives are to be surrendered to the Lord, they must be fully surrendered.

Don't stand on the outskirts of salvation, simply peering in because you like what it stands for. Take the challenge to give all to the Lord; this is the only way to taste abundant life in Him. Everyone wants to be a winner, but not everyone wants to make the sacrifices necessary to become a winner. It's only those who make sacrifices and train for the race who eventually cross the finish line in the end.

Even though God desires us to fully surrender our lives and give Him our "all," we need to be careful that we never fall into the trap of thinking that hard work—or even our act of surrender, in and of itself—can earn salvation. This is the mistake that the rich young ruler made. When he asked Jesus what "good thing" he could do to inherit salvation, Jesus laid out the facts:

> *Thou shalt do no murder, Thou shalt not commit adultery, Thou shalt not steal, Thou shalt not bear false witness, Honour thy father and thy mother: and, Thou shalt love thy neighbour as thyself.* (Matthew 19:18–19)

Don't come into the body of Christ and become witless. If you had good gifts that you used for the world, you need to sharpen those gifts for the kingdom.

The rich ruler, in his pride, said he had upheld these laws all his life. He knew he had a deficiency—or else why would He have asked Jesus this question in the first place?—but he refused to acknowledge his own spiritual bankruptcy.

Jesus wanted to impress upon this man that God's high standards were impossible for man to uphold. There is no way this man could have satisfied all the Lord's commandments, for *"all have sinned, and come short of the glory of God"* (Romans 3:23). Perhaps he upheld the letter of the law by remaining faithful to his wife, obedient to his parents, and honest to his neighbors; but if his heart was not right, he failed to uphold the spirit of the law and therefore sinned:

Ye have heard that it was said by them of old time, Thou shalt not kill; and whosoever shall kill shall be in danger of the judgment: but I say unto you, That whosoever is angry with his brother without a cause shall be in danger of the judgment....Ye have heard that it was said by them of old time, Thou shalt not commit adultery: but I say unto you, That whosoever looketh on a woman to lust after her hath committed adultery with her already in his heart....Ye have heard that it hath been said, An eye for an eye, and a tooth for a tooth: but I say unto you, That ye resist not evil: but whosoever shall smite thee on thy right cheek, turn to him the other also....Ye have heard that it hath been said, Thou shalt love thy neighbour, and hate thine enemy. But I say unto you, Love your enemies, bless them that curse you, do good to them that hate you, and pray for them which despitefully use you, and persecute you.
(Matthew 5:21–22, 27–28, 38–39, 43–44)

You can go through the motions by attending church on Sunday, paying your tithes, singing wonderful choruses, or weekly serving at a soup kitchen; but until you acknowledge your need for Christ over everything else, you're suffering from spiritual bankruptcy.

You cannot meet God's standards through your own good works. Your righteousness is nothing compared to the Lord's: *"But we are all as an unclean thing, and all our righteousnesses are as filthy rags; and we all do fade as a leaf; and our iniquities, like the wind, have taken us away"* (Isaiah 64:6). We cannot please His righteous requirements or satisfy His perfect justice in our own strength. We are saved only through His grace, nothing else. Don't be like the rich young ruler. Instead, recognize your spiritual shortcomings. Fall on your face in surrender as you accept God's good and gracious gifts.

He Knows Your Needs

Are you holding on to your wealth? Are you bypassing God's good eternal treasures because you're too busy gripping on to the things of this world? There's no need to do this, for the Lord knows your needs and desires even better than you do yourself.

> *Therefore take no thought, saying, What shall we eat? or, What shall we drink? or, Wherewithal shall we be clothed? (for after all these things do the Gentiles seek:) for your heavenly Father knoweth that ye have need of all these things. But seek ye first the kingdom of God, and his righteousness; and all these things shall be added unto you.*
>
> (Matthew 6:31–33)

God knows what you have need of. He knows your physical needs, your emotional needs, your mental needs, your spiritual needs. He hears your stomach before it even growls and tastes your tears before they fall. He sees your stressful days before they happen and anticipates the times you'll need an extra dose of patience. He knows you inside and out. *"The very hairs of your head are all numbered"* (Matthew 10:30). Along with this intimacy comes a knowledge of your needs. He knows what you need.

"Take no thought for these things," He says, "for I know your needs, and I've got it all under control. *'Set your affection on things above, not on things on the earth'* (Colossians 3:2). There is no need for you to worry; I'll supply your physical, emotional, mental, and spiritual needs according to My perfect timing. Seek Me alone. I will provide for you."

When you seek the Lord, receive His Spirit, and start walking in His ways, your measure of faith becomes uncontainable. You are able to stop worrying about your wealth and let God supply your needs instead. The joy of the Lord radiates through you until you can hardly contain the good news of His perfect provision. Like Jeremiah, you say *"But his word was in mine heart as a burning fire shut up in my bones"* (Jeremiah 20:9). Your joy is uncontainable.

God seeks broken spirits and contrite hearts from His people. He desires your whole self, surrendered to Him and ready for His good will. This is where God's finest, which surpasses all earthly wealth, is to be found and enjoyed. This is where eternal, heavenly treasures abound. *"Lay not up for yourselves treasures upon earth, where moth and rust doth corrupt, and where thieves break through and steal"* (Matthew 6:19). God knows your every need. Will you let Him provide? His promises and provisions are not for this world only, but for eternal gain. Abandon whatever you're placing before God; start tasting His everlasting fruit today.

Chapter Five

His Covenant People

Chapter 5

His Covenant People

f you're a Christian, you've been rescued. God has saved us all from our capsized ships amidst stormy seas. Some of us were even submerged, nearly drowned in the depths of sin and death; but we are His covenant people, chosen from the start of time to be rescued and redeemed. Before Adam and Eve tasted that apple in the garden—even before they were created!—God knew that mankind would sin and fall away from Him. But instead of leaving us for dead in sin's stormy seas, God sent out a Rescuer.

That's where the expression "I've been *saved* by the blood of the Lamb" comes from. God has *saved* us, through the shed blood of His perfect Son, from the sinfulness that once engulfed us. We are no longer aimless vessels or shipwrecked boats that must fear destruction with every rising wave. As His people, we have been rescued from life's biggest storm—sin. We are now in covenant with the great Redeemer, and He is committed to bringing us through the rest of life's storms.

As a young boy growing up, I remember hearing my dad say, "God is still looking for a yielded vessel." Earlier in this book, we talked about being yielded *vessels*, or *containers*, in which the Lord could manifest His Spirit. *Vessel* can also mean "a watercraft," and God desires us to be yielded vessels in this sense, too. How so? It's like this: Even though He's rescued you from sin, the biggest storm, you're still on the waters, facing waves and high water every day. When you are a yielded *vessel*, you're like a willing ship, eager for the Savior to pilot you through life's waves.

Instead of leaving us for dead in sin's stormy seas, God sent out a Rescuer.

This is what God desires: our commitment to let Him be Captain of our ships. And who better to commit to and trust than God? Who is more faithful, more powerful, more loving, more perfect? No one! Not one person can compare to Him. It is an honor to be chosen by Him as His covenant people. Let us lovingly return commitment unto Him; let us give Him the steering wheels of our vessels.

God's Rescue Mission

Before the Lord rescued me, I didn't have direction; my life was certainly an aimless craft on the sea. First of all, I was out of touch with reality. Like all non-Christians, I didn't feel remorse for the things I should have. As long as a person is out of fellowship with God, he's out of fellowship with his conscience. I was out of fellowship with my conscience. I would do and say certain things that I wouldn't even think about doing or saying today. And it wouldn't bother me one bit. It bothered God—in fact, it angered and saddened Him—but it didn't bother me at all.

When He saved me, however, I became aware of all the sin in my life. I felt so bad for all the wrong I had done, and I wanted to do something to help appease all the guilt I felt. I remembered that God desires us to serve others, and so I started doing as much as I could to help other people. I knew what God wanted me to do: He wanted me to pick up the broom and sweep the church floor; He wanted me to pick up the toilet brush and clean the commodes. Some people have said to me, "You should have gone to school and tried to get your life together." But I felt the Lord telling me to serve others at that time.

Part of me felt that if I did enough good things, I could have some peace of mind. God has since shown me that it is only His grace, not my good works, that grants me salvation and provides me with peace. My salvation isn't contingent on good works or on helping people. It comes only because God has chosen to graciously forgive me and because I have chosen to accept His forgiveness by faith. But even though works do not save us, God still desires our acts of loving service.

> *What doth it profit, my brethren, though a man say he hath faith, and have not works? can faith save him? If a brother or sister be naked, and destitute of daily food, and one of you say unto them, Depart in peace, be ye warmed and filled; notwithstanding ye give them not those things which are needful to the body; what doth it profit? Even so faith, if it hath not works, is dead, being alone.* (James 2:14–17)

Sometimes, when we are disconnected from God, and thus from reality, we waste our lives. This is what I did for many years, until God rescued me. I didn't know how He was going to turn things around when I first came to Him, but I had a confidence that He would. And He did. He has filled my life here on earth with amazing spiritual blessings and I know I have a wonderful eternity in heaven to look forward to.

When I look at where I am today and consider where I was before, I am amazed. Nobody prepped and primed me for a good life, and I certainly wasn't born with a silver spoon in my mouth. No, I know what it means to be out in the street, to be on drugs, to live a life of lies and deception. When I came to God, my life was a mess. But our God is an awesome God! He can take a man off the streets, clean him up, advance him, and put his life in fast forward.

Safe in His Arms

When I came into relationship with God, I came into a right relationship with myself. Many people have been tormented by lack of confidence in themselves, by fear of failure, or by feelings of worthlessness. Oftentimes, they seek to forget their insecurities through drugs, alcohol, or other temporary "solutions" that suppress real-life struggles. However, these suppressants are not what the Great Physician ordered. Jesus Christ has a more perfect and permanent remedy—Himself.

Before you met Jesus, you were like a little child, seeking protection, comfort, nourishment, and peace from the arms of anyone you felt might help you. Once you were reunited with your heavenly Father, you began feeling safe and at peace. No person or thing can ever care for you as perfectly as your heavenly Father does. He alone can quiet your cries and satisfy your soul. You, as God's covenant child, are safe in the arms of your great and mighty Father.

Since He is your Father, He knows what you need. Just as all good parents know their children's needs, your heavenly Father knows your needs. He knows your needs even better than you do. Have you ever noticed how children sometimes think they know what they need when they really don't? My daughter, for instance, used to throw temper tantrums whenever it was time for her afternoon nap. She hated taking naps and would fight tooth and nail to get out of it. The irony was that she was so cranky because she needed a nap. The very nap that she would so grumpily protest was exactly what she needed to get rid of her grumpiness. My wife and I, as her parents, knew what our daughter needed better than she did herself.

Before you met Jesus, you were like a little child, seeking protection, comfort, nourishment, and peace from the arms of anyone you felt might help you.

It's the same with our heavenly Father. He knows our spiritual, emotional, mental, and physical needs even better than we do ourselves. And since He loves us and is committed to us as His children, He provides for those needs. Often, we will disagree with what He determines are our needs, just as my daughter disagreed about the necessity of naps. But no matter what, we must accept on faith that He is a perfect and loving parent. We must allow Him to provide for us, even when His provisions are momentarily painful:

> For whom the Lord loveth he chasteneth, and scour-geth every son whom he receiveth. If ye endure chas-tening, God dealeth with you as with sons; for what son is he whom the father chasteneth not? But if ye be without chastisement, whereof all are partakers, then are ye bastards, and not sons. Furthermore we have had fathers of our flesh which corrected us, and we gave them reverence: shall we not much rather be in subjection unto the Father of spirits, and live? For they verily for a few days chastened us after their own

pleasure; but he for our profit, that we might be par-
takers of his holiness. (Hebrews 12:6–10)

Our Response: Loving Commitment

We've already talked about our Father's perfect commitment. Because He loves us as His covenant children, He is committed to carrying out wonderful things in our lives, for His glory and our good. *"And we know that all things work together for good to them that love God, to them who are the called according to his purpose"* (Romans 8:28). God wants you to taste the good things He has for you. He wants you to live and not die, to be blessed and not cursed. The best thing you can do is open yourself up to those blessings by living a life of obedience to the Lord. If you submit to His discipline, the benefits will be glorious; but if you resist His discipline, you are your own biggest hindrance.

Submitting to God's discipline is how you show Him that you love Him. When you let the Lord steer your life's ship, you demonstrate your love and commitment to Him. He, in turn, is able to manifest the heights and depths of His love by gently commanding your "yielded vessel," or your life.

One thing God desires whenever He asks for our obedience is a love and commitment fashioned after His own. God's love should be the pattern we follow whenever we show love to others. Mankind's love is naturally conditional and imperfect; oftentimes, we show love to others only because they show love to us first. But as soon as those whom we "love" upset us, we suddenly feel unloving and begin to treat them unlovingly. Our love is based on reciprocity; whatever we get, we give in return. As soon as someone is cruel to us, we have the hardest time loving them back, even though Jesus has commanded us to *"love your enemies, bless them that curse you, do good to them that hate you, and pray for them which despitefully use you, and persecute you"* (Matthew 5:44). God's love, however, is perfect and unconditional, for it is built upon commitment. He has decided that He is going to love us, and no matter what we do to upset Him, He will still always love us.

Romans 5:8 says that *"while we were yet sinners, Christ died for us."* This is extreme love, agape love, perfect love. Christ loved you when you were a gang member, when you were a crack addict, when you were strung out on dope and out of touch with everything around you. He loved you when you didn't even love yourself. That's the kind of love that Jesus has for the sinner. His love is so rich that even after He gets you out of a mess and you get into that same mess again, He still loves you. He doesn't abandon you; He embraces you. He doesn't cut you off; He corrects you. And He doesn't leave you; He leads you. *"He hath said, I will never leave thee, nor forsake thee"* (Hebrews 13:5).

That's the kind of love God has for His children. And that's the kind of love we need to demonstrate in our own lives. Commitment needs to be at its core. Without commitment, love is based on feeling, and this will always be fickle and bound for failure. Decide now if you are willing to *commit* to love, no matter how difficult it may be to show that love. Can you say to God, "I'll love You, even when I don't feel Your presence in my life. I'll love You, even when Your discipline hurts"? Can you say to those around you, "I'll love you, even when you upset me. I'll love you, even when you make me mad"? Love like this does not fail, for it is based on commitment.

When you become a person of commitment, everyone can see it. Not only are you committed to the people in your life, but you're also committed to your job, your church, and all aspects of your life. People of commitment are people of *wholistic commitment*. They develop attitudes of commitment that permeate all areas of their lives.

When God sees your commitment, He often forms a supernatural passageway leading to your intended end. "Because you were committed in your heart," He says, "I'm going to give you a shortcut. I'm going to bless you to accomplish in two years what would ordinarily take five years to achieve." This doesn't always happen, but often it does for those who are committed to working hard. *"He becometh poor that dealeth with a slack hand: but the hand of the diligent maketh rich"* (Proverbs 10:4). That is why I emphasize the importance of a healthy work ethic; exhibiting good work ethics now often hastens the promotion of tomorrow.

No commitment equals no return.

Your work ethic involves the law of commitment. When you are committed to a company, a company commits itself to you. When you come to work on time, stay your full eight hours, and work hard every weekday, your boss is happy and shows it through the pay he gives you, the vacation days he allows you to have, and the promotions that will occasionally come along. Commitment seldom goes unrewarded.

The law of commitment works both ways; when you don't show commitment, you don't experience the benefits that come with commitment. No commitment equals no return. Sometimes, the consequences are downright unpleasant. I find it hard to take people seriously who continually show up late for work. When they're fired, they always have an excuse. "See, Pastor," they say, "the supervisor was jealous of me." "Really?" I think to myself. "Companies normally fire people for valid reasons."

Only rarely do people get fired simply because their bosses don't like them. In fact, I worked a job once where a man didn't like me. He would bring lunch to work for everyone, but he would never bring lunch for me. Since my work was so efficient, however, all he could say was, "He's a good worker." When it was promotion time, I was the first one considered. Your bosses don't have to like you; they just have to know you're a hard and serious worker.

When people see the value you place on commitment, they realize that anything you do will be done well. When you value commitment in your heart, you're going to be reliable and determined to see your tasks to fruition, no matter what they may be. Are you committed? Would others consider you to be a person of commitment? Or are you just partially committed, exerting your best effort only when you stand to gain from it?

Because He Lives, Let Us Love

Beloved, let us love one another: for love is of God; and every one that loveth is born of God, and knoweth God. (1 John 4:7)

In His Word, God gives us special instructions on how we are to love each other as brothers and sisters in Christ. When you're part of the church, you're part of an organization, or a collection of people devoted to a common purpose. But even more importantly, you are part of an organism.

For as the body is one, and hath many members, and all the members of that one body, being many, are one body: so also is Christ. For by one Spirit are we all baptized into one body, whether we be Jews or Gentiles, whether we be bond or free; and have been all made to drink into one Spirit. For the body is not one member, but many. (1 Corinthians 12:12–14)

We are all parts of the body of Christ, each one a different member with a different purpose.

If the foot shall say, Because I am not the hand, I am not of the body; is it therefore not of the body? And if the ear shall say, Because I am not the eye, I am not of the body; is it therefore not of the body? If the whole body were an eye, where were the hearing? If the whole were hearing, where were the smelling? But now hath God set the members every one of them in the body, as it hath pleased him. And if they were all one member, where were the body? But now are they many members, yet but one body.

(1 Corinthians 12:15–20)

As these verses show, every church member is different from the others, but just as important. If the eyes of a human body were to stop working, that body could not function to its full potential. The body of Christ is the same way; it cannot carry out its purpose without all of its parts. The health of every member is essential.

This is where love comes in. For the body of Christ to remain healthy and functioning, its parts need to work together. When the left ankle is sprained, the right ankle works double time to bear the body's weight. Or when the right eye is swollen shut, the left eye takes care of all the seeing until its partner is healed. In the church, we must do the same. In love, we must bear each other's burdens. Not only this, we must encourage each other, too, which helps prevent heartache and hurt. Just as a runner can avoid injury by stretching her muscles, warming up before races, and not overworking her body during practice, we can avoid injury in the body of Christ by taking precautionary measures as well. This involves lifting each other up in prayer, training in the Word together, and helping each other in life's day-to-day struggles.

Are you living in an organism or merely an organization? The two are similar. Each is a collection of people devoted to a common purpose or end. An organism, however, is more than just a "collection" of people; it is a unified assemblage, a living whole, a breathing body. There is life in the organism that the organization will never know. I don't want to be part of an organization; I want to be part of a living, breathing organism. I don't want to be a church member; I want to be part of the body of Christ. What about you? Are you ready to push beyond organizational structures and into the realm of real life?

Before you entered into a relationship with Christ, you may have envied the blessings you saw in the lives of Christians around you. You wanted the joy and peace that they had. You couldn't understand why such good things were missing from your life. Perhaps non-Christians look at your life the same way today. "How come he's so blessed?" they might ask, or, "How come she's so joyful?"

Are you living in an organism or merely an organization?

Such people may feel jealousy, passionately wishing they could have the same gifts in their lives. Their view is blocked by covetousness while envious suspicion clouds their vision. They think you're playing some sort of religious game and not really living a life of holiness. They think all the "good fruit" in your life (see Galatians 5:22–23) can't be real. "That fruit is fake," they say. "It must all be made of wax."

Unfortunately, such envious suspicion also happens *within* the church body. Do you know what I'm talking about? Perhaps you've felt jealousy as you examined spiritual gifts in the lives of fellow believers. Maybe you've wished for your harvest of spiritual goods to be the biggest in the orchard. Perhaps you've even longed for hardships to fall on your brothers and sisters so that their spiritual fruits would not seem so sweet.

Such attitudes have been around for a long time. Jesus described a similar situation in His parable of the Prodigal Son.

Now his elder son was in the field: and as he came and drew nigh to the house, he heard music and dancing. And he called one of the servants, and asked what these things meant. And he said unto him, Thy brother is come; and thy father hath killed the fatted calf, because he hath received him safe and sound. And he was angry, and would not go in.
(Luke 15:25–28)

Jealousy, envy, and bitterness are neither Christlike nor loving. As God's chosen covenant people, we are united into one body, which is Christ. Feelings of resentment do nothing to unify the body; instead, they shatter its wholeness. Let's not envy the blessings in each other's lives or be angry at the treasures God provides for others, but rather praise God for the miracles He works in the lives of all His children. This is where real relationship with Christ begins and mere religion ends.

Eternal Commitment

Commitment isn't always convenient. Sometimes, it is downright difficult, especially during hardships. But no matter how hard it is, commitment is a necessity, for some of life's greatest lessons are learned only through adversity. It is during the tough times that God teaches some of His greatest lessons. If we are to fully receive these lessons, we must remain committed to the Teacher and steadfast until the end.

*Therefore being justified by faith, we have peace with God through our Lord Jesus Christ: by whom also we have access by faith into this grace wherein we stand, and rejoice in hope of the glory of God. And not only so, but **we glory in tribulations also: knowing that tribulation worketh patience; and patience, experience; and experience, hope: and hope maketh not ashamed;** because the love of*

God is shed abroad in our hearts by the Holy Ghost which is given unto us.
                              (Romans 5:1–5, emphasis added)

When we're committed enough to yield to the Lord, no matter how trying the circumstances, we lay the groundwork for future blessings. It is during these tribulations that the Lord strengthens our relationships with Him, and it is in the fire that He purifies our faith:

Wherein ye greatly rejoice, though now for a season, if need be, ye are in heaviness through manifold temptations: that the trial of your faith, being much more precious than of gold that perisheth, though it be tried with fire, might be found unto praise and honour and glory at the appearing of Jesus Christ.
                              (1 Peter 1:6–7)

Staying committed during the hard times is tough. You maybe be tempted to throw in the towel and give up the whole Christian fight. I encourage you to remember these two points whenever you're struggling:

1. Your struggles are short-lived in the scope of eternity.

2. Your struggles will blossom into blessings as the Lord waters them with His grace.

If ye endure chastening, God dealeth with you as with sons; for what son is he whom the father chasteneth not? But if ye be without chastisement, whereof all are partakers, then are ye bastards, and not sons. Furthermore we have had fathers of our flesh which corrected us, and we gave them reverence: shall we not much rather be in subjection unto the Father of spirits, and live? For they verily for a few days chastened us after their own pleasure; but he for our profit, that we might be partakers of his holiness.

Now no chastening for the present seemeth to be joyous, but grievous: nevertheless afterward it yieldeth the peaceable fruit of righteousness unto them which are exercised thereby. (Hebrews 12:7–11)

Sometimes, when people face struggles and hardships, they think God is out to get them. Nothing is further from the truth. While it's true that our hardships often are the result of sin, God always uses our struggles for His glory and our good. *"And we know that all things work together for good to them that love God, to them who are the called according to his purpose"* (Romans 8:28). So, the next time you feel disheartened because of all the difficulties in your life, remember that God will ultimately use them for His awesome and unfathomable eternal plan.

Commitment isn't always convenient, but it's a necessity.

One of the easiest blessings to spot during adversity is the strengthening of your relationship with the Lord God Himself. When everything in your life is going smoothly and not a hardship is to be found, do you seek the Lord? Most people have a difficult time faithfully following Him whenever life is okay. When things get difficult, however, it's a lot easier to come to Him. In fact, we feel almost forced to come to Him as we realize our own weaknesses. When things are easy, we often don't seek God as we should. But when all hell breaks loose, we're eager to look to Him for help. It is during these times that God works His most wonderful miracles. Let's not hide from hardship but instead thank God for what He will do through it. Let us pray, too, that we will be committed to letting Him sculpt us and that we will be always ready for His refining fire.

A Personal Reality Check

As Christians, our number one commitment should be to God and God alone. If we were to make lists, in descending order, of all the priorities in our lives, He should always come first. Every other commitment should follow after commitment to God; other concerns should be simply derivatives of the primary concern, which is obedience to the Lord.

But you know the story: We're sinners, and we let things slip out of order quickly. Can you claim that God is always your number one commitment? I know I can't! So often I find my own selfish desires and wants taking precedence over my commitment to God. It's during these times that God has to send me little "reality checks" to remind me where my focus should be.

This happened to me not too long ago. There were some people who decided to change membership from the church I pastor, for what I thought were very frivolous reasons. This stressed me out. I started worrying and fretting about it so much that I took my eyes off God. Pretty soon, the situation was consuming me, and I had let God slip from His number one spot on my commitment list. Instead, I was focused on my own popularity; I spent all my energy wondering how I could win those people back. God wouldn't have this. He knows His rightful place, and He wasn't going to let me keep bumping Him down the list. He wasn't going to let me worry about my own image and totally forget His. "Guess what?" He said to me. "You're not irreplaceable. If you leave tomorrow, I'll raise somebody else up to take your place. And I'll work through them in a mighty way, because I am God and I will always see My plan to fruition. So, stop complaining, and turn your attention to the tasks I've set before you."

At first, I was taken aback. "Doesn't He have some nerve," I thought. "He's telling me, the *pastor,* that He doesn't need me? Doesn't He know how much I've done, how much time I've given, and how many people I've helped? And He says He doesn't need me?"

"That's right," God said. "I don't need you."

When I finally grasped this truth, it delivered me. Of course God didn't need me. He could use anyone or anything to complete His work! Instead of complaining and worrying about my own image, I decided it was time to let God be my number one commitment again. He was going to keep the church running, whether I was in it or not. This was reality—He didn't need me; I needed Him.

What Is Your Level of Commitment?

Is the Lord trying to send *you* a reality check? Have you let Him slip from His number one spot like I did? Or, like the rich young ruler of Matthew 19, have you always placed God lower than number one on your list? Either way, it's probably time for a reality check.

Remember, there's no question about our Lord's faithfulness or commitment. His Word and all of history resound with promises of commitment to His children. We find one of these promises in Leviticus 26:12, when God said to the Israelites, *"And I will walk among you, and will be your God, and ye shall be my people."* God continued to use this language of commitment—*"your God"* and *"my people"*—throughout the Old Testament. (See Isaiah 40:1; Jeremiah 7:23; 30:22; Ezekiel 36:28; Joel 2:26–27.) In sending His Son to *"walk among* [us]" and reclaim us as "[His] *people,"* He fulfilled this commitment. There is no question that the Lord God is committed to His children.

The real question is, Are we committed to Him? This is where the rubber meets the road, where God conducts His reality checks, where we're forced to evaluate our own levels of faithfulness and commitment. What is your level of commitment?

In the final section of this chapter, we'll break down the elements of commitment to see what it looks like. But before we do that, let's consider what commitment is *not*. There's a lot of confusion out there about what commitment looks like. Before we grow in commitment to our Lord, we need to reject any misconceptions we have about commitment.

First of all, commitment is more than just words. True, commitment does require your statements of faith and devotion. *"That if thou shalt confess with thy mouth the Lord Jesus, and shalt believe in thine heart that God hath raised him from the dead, thou shalt be saved"* (Romans 10:9). Commitment extends beyond mere words, however; it shows itself through acts of faithfulness and good works.

> *What doth it profit, my brethren, though a man say he hath faith, and have not works? can faith save him? If a brother or sister be naked, and destitute of daily food, and one of you say unto them, Depart in peace, be ye warmed and filled; notwithstanding ye give them not those things which are needful to the body; what doth it profit? Even so faith, if it hath not works, is dead, being alone. Yea, a man may say, Thou hast faith, and I have works: show me thy faith without thy works, and I will show thee my faith by my works. Thou believest that there is one God; thou doest well: the devils also believe, and tremble. But wilt thou know, O vain man, that faith without works is dead? was not Abraham our father justified by works, when he had offered Isaac his son upon the altar? seest thou how faith wrought with his works, and by works was faith made perfect? And the scripture was fulfilled which saith, Abraham believed God, and it was imputed unto him for righteousness: and*

he was called the Friend of God. Ye see then how
that by works a man is justified, and not by faith only.
(James 2:14–24)

In other words, you can talk and talk and talk about how committed you are to the Lord. But until you show it through action, you're nothing but talk. A commitment of words is no commitment at all.

True commitment extends beyond mere words; it shows itself through acts of faithfulness and good works.

In addition, commitment is not a flashy show for the purpose of getting other people's attention. You know what I'm talking about; maybe you've even done it yourself. I'm talking about jumping around in church, lifting your hands in the air during praise time, carrying the biggest Bible you can find, and wearing nothing but Christian T-shirts simply for the purpose of turning heads. True commitment doesn't care if others see. The truly committed person is content with quiet prayer in the closet:

And when thou prayest, thou shalt not be as the hypo-
crites are: for they love to pray standing in the syna-
gogues and in the corners of the streets, that they may
be seen of men. Verily I say unto you, They have their
reward. But thou, when thou prayest, enter into thy
closet, and when thou hast shut thy door, pray to thy
Father which is in secret; and thy Father which seeth
in secret shall reward thee openly. (Matthew 6:5–6)

The truly committed person doesn't make a big show for others to see when he's fasting:

Moreover when ye fast, be not, as the hypocrites, of a sad countenance: for they disfigure their faces, that they may appear unto men to fast. Verily I say unto you, They have their reward. But thou, when thou fastest, anoint thine head, and wash thy face; that thou appear not unto men to fast, but unto thy Father which is in secret: and thy Father, which seeth in secret, shall reward thee openly. (Matthew 6:16–18)

Finally, the truly committed person keeps his gift-giving a secret:

Take heed that ye do not your alms before men, to be seen of them: otherwise ye have no reward of your Father which is in heaven. Therefore when thou doest thine alms, do not sound a trumpet before thee, as the hypocrites do in the synagogues and in the streets, that they may have glory of men. Verily I say unto you, They have their reward. But when thou doest alms, let not thy left hand know what thy right hand doeth: that thine alms may be in secret: and thy Father which seeth in secret himself shall reward thee openly. (Matthew 6:1–4)

True commitment does involve good works, because merely *saying* we are committed to the Lord means nothing. He calls us to show our love through acts of faithfulness. These good works, however, must never be intended as attention-grabbers. Whenever we do our good works, they should be for God's glory alone, not our own.

What is your level of commitment?

The Nature of Commitment

The powerful challenge to you as a believer is this: Can you be committed to God unconditionally? When you haven't gotten a raise in months, your bills are piling up, and everyone else around you is prospering, will you stay committed?

When you're in the midst of family fights, church quarrels, or workplace battles, will you stick it out? When you've had the flu for a week and it just won't go away, will you remain devoted?

Anybody can be committed when his life is overflowing with gifts. Any person can stay faithful when her life is running smoothly. But I believe that God has a way of testing and trying our commitment, and this involves hardship. When burdens take the place of physical gifts, and silence replaces words of comfort, will we show commitment?

"Therefore shall ye keep my commandments, and do them: I am the LORD" (Leviticus 22:31). Notice that God didn't say, "Keep my commandments when you feel like it" or "Keep my commandments if it makes you happy." Nor did He say, "Keep my commandments when it's easy to do so" or "Keep my commandments only if it doesn't cause too much trouble." No! He says, *"Keep my commandments."* Period. There are no ifs, ands, or buts about it. He wants our commitment, no matter what.

Below are a few guidelines for faithfulness, or pointers on how you can practically carry out commitment in your life. They are:

- Develop versatility
- Accept those things which you cannot change
- Remember the Lord's provisions

Let's take a look at each of these in closer detail.

Versatility

When you're committed to God, you need to possess versatility. *Versatility* means being flexible enough to handle the unexpected twists and turns on the path of life. The word *versatile* itself comes from a Latin word, *versare*, meaning "to turn." So, when life sends you curve balls, you need to be versatile enough to respond without panicking; this is commitment.

> God has a way of testing and trying
> our commitment, and this
> often involves hardship.

Every day is not filled with sunshine; there will be many cloudy days. But neither is life always glum, gloomy, and rainy; you will have your sunshine, too. Can you take these ups and downs? Can you commit to praying, no matter what the weather, or to reading your Bible, no matter what your mood? The committed person must be versatile and willing to practice commitment in any and all situations.

Inevitably, situations will arise in life that will concern and depress us, making commitment the last thing we want to practice. But we must understand that our relationship with God is independent of these ups and downs. Whether something *feels* good or bad, God's using it to work together for our good. *"And we know that all things work together for good to them that love God, to them who are the called according to his purpose"* (Romans 8:28). Whether everything in life is going great or terribly, we need to be versatile enough to remain steadfast to the Lord.

Acceptance

The second guideline for commitment is accepting those things that we cannot change. This goes hand in hand with versatility. Oftentimes, when life is tough, we spend lots of energy trying to make things better, even if the situation is entirely out of our control. The serenity prayer, which you may have heard, holds a great bit of wisdom for circumstances such as this. It says,

*God, grant me the Serenity
to accept the things I cannot change,
the Courage to change the things I can,
and the Wisdom to know the difference.*

*Living one day at a time;
Enjoying one moment at a time;
Accepting hardship as the
pathway to peace.*

*Taking, as He did, this
sinful world as it is,
not as I would have it.*

*Trusting that He will make
all things right if I
surrender to His Will;*

*That I may be reasonably happy
in this life, and supremely
happy with Him forever in
the next. Amen. **

You've probably heard the first few lines of the prayer but may not be familiar with the rest of it. I'd like for us to take a look at the whole prayer because it relates to our discussion about commitment.

"God grant me the serenity to accept the things I cannot change." This is important. There are some things in life that we simply do not have control over. For example, you can work extra hard at your job and be extremely nice to your boss, but if he doesn't like you, there's nothing you can

* *Serenity Prayer.* Taken from the Minnesota Recovery Page, accessed at http://www.lakeweb1.com/mrp/literature/Serenity.htm.

do about it. You can't *make* someone like you, just as you can't turn back time or change the weather. Some things are simply out of our control, and we waste lots of precious energy if we try controlling these uncontrollables. Does this mean we should ignore these situations? Not at all! If your boss doesn't like you, you can do all that's in your power to make him like you. And, most importantly, you can surrender the situation to God in prayer. When you do this, pray also for an extra dose of acceptance. Pray that you would have the peace of mind to stay faithful, committed, and devoted to the Lord in the midst of situations you cannot change.

One thing that I find helpful in learning acceptance is to praise God for the things I do have. For example, someone could pray, "Lord, I wish my nose wasn't so big. Then I'd be a lot better looking." Or instead, that person could choose to accept the nose God provided by thanking Him for the ability to breathe through it. *"Rejoice in the Lord alway: and again I say, Rejoice"* (Philippians 4:4). When you learn to accept God's will and praise Him always, then you will be able to fully appreciate and enjoy the good things He provides. Learn to accept those things that you were never meant to change.

"Courage to change the things I can, and the wisdom to know the difference." On the opposite end of acceptance is apathy. Do you know what apathy is? It means simply not caring one bit what happens. This happens when you take acceptance too far. People who are perfectly capable of working but instead lie around doing nothing all day, might say, "I'm not lazy. I've just come to accept that I'm not a very motivated person." This isn't acceptance; this is apathy. You see, the Lord only calls us to accept the things that we cannot change. The things that we can change, however, we better start changing. If you and your brother haven't talked for years, and you know you need to apologize, then why don't you apologize?

> *Therefore if thou bring thy gift to the altar, and there rememberest that thy brother hath ought against thee; leave there thy gift before the altar, and go thy way; first be reconciled to thy brother, and then come and offer thy gift.* (Matthew 5:23–24)

If you have a habit of swearing or of misusing the Lord's name, then why don't you try to stop that habit?

> *Thou shalt not take the name of the LORD thy God in vain; for the LORD will not hold him guiltless that taketh his name in vain.* (Exodus 20:7)

> *Let no corrupt communication proceed out of your mouth, but that which is good to the use of edifying, that it may minister grace unto the hearers.* (Ephesians 4:29)

Whatever we can't change, we must accept.
But those things that we can change,
we need to pray for courage
to change them.

Whatever we can't change, we must accept. But those things that we can change, we need to pray for courage to change them. And where do we get the "wisdom to know the difference" between the two? Most importantly, in God's Word. Scripture is our primary source for knowing the things He desires. Study God's Word so that you may know His will. Whatever He commands, those are the things He wants you to work on changing in your life. It should be your goal to daily bring your life closer and closer to matching the standards in His Word.

"Living one day at a time; enjoying one moment at a time; accepting hardship as the pathway to peace." Commitment is a daily decision, not just a one-time event. Sure, there is a point in all Christians' lives when they choose to make the first "big" commitment; this is when they ask Christ to be their Savior and Lord. They commit their lives, from that point onward, to Christ. But commitment can't stop there. As this portion of the serenity prayer reminds us, we always need to live "one day at a time"—which may mean recommitting on a daily basis. *"If any man will come after me, let him deny himself, and take up his cross daily, and follow me"* (Luke 9:23). As sinful human beings, we easily forget our commitment to the Lord. It is good to review it often.

Notice the second half of this section: "accepting hardship as the pathway to peace." As we discussed earlier, trials and adversity are often God's greatest tools for bringing blessing into our lives. This is a good reminder that true peace requires us to accept hardship first.

"Taking, as He did, this sinful world as it is, not as I would have it." This portion of the prayer reminds us again that we must accept those things that we cannot change. Until the Lord returns, there will always be sin in this world. We must accept this and not get frustrated whenever life is imperfect. Remember, life will never be perfect until the Lord's return. It is only then that we will be content with the way things are and fully able to accept our circumstances without any reservations.

> *And I heard a great voice out of heaven saying, Behold, the tabernacle of God is with men, and he will dwell with them, and they shall be his people, and God himself shall be with them, and be their God. And God shall wipe away all tears from their eyes; and there shall be no more death, neither sorrow, nor crying, neither shall there be any more pain: for the former things are passed away.*
>
> (Revelation 21:3–4)

Until the Lord's return, we have to accept the sinful condition of this world. We don't have to be happy about it—the Lord certainly isn't!—but we have to accept it as fact. We only fool ourselves if we pretend that we, in our own efforts, can make a perfect world. No matter how good our lives on this earth may be, they will always be like garbage compared to the wonderful eternity in heaven that awaits us.

"Trusting that He will make all things right if I surrender to His Will; that I may be reasonably happy in this life, and supremely happy with Him forever in the next. Amen." The closing portion of the serenity prayer reminds us that acceptance is necessary for us to experience peace and happiness. If we do not surrender to the Lord by accepting those things that we can't change, then our hearts will be burdened and unhappy. But when we accept His will, we are freed to taste true peace and joy. Don't let life's difficulties prevent you from knowing God's joys. Accept life's struggles and praise Him that they are only temporary. Be joyful that there will be no more tears in heaven. An eternal perspective like this makes it a lot easier to accept temporary hardships.

Provision

The final guideline for commitment is remembering the Lord's provisions. It's easy to stay committed to the Lord when you know that He is so committed to you. Consider some of these Scripture verses about the Lord's commitment to provide for our needs:

> *Thou visitest the earth, and waterest it: thou greatly enrichest it with the river of God, which is full of water: thou preparest them corn, when thou hast so provided for it.* (Psalm 65:9)

> *Therefore I say unto you, Take no thought for your life, what ye shall eat, or what ye shall drink; nor yet for your body, what ye shall put on. Is not the life more*

than meat, and the body than raiment? Behold the fowls of the air: for they sow not, neither do they reap, nor gather into barns; yet your heavenly Father feedeth them. Are ye not much better than they? which of you by taking thought can add one cubit unto his stature? and why take ye thought for rai-ment? Consider the lilies of the field, how they grow; they toil not, neither do they spin: and yet I say unto you, That even Solomon in all his glory was not arrayed like one of these. Wherefore, if God so clothe the grass of the field, which to day is, and to morrow is cast into the oven, shall he not much more clothe you, O ye of little faith? Therefore take no thought, saying, What shall we eat? or, What shall we drink? or, Wherewithal shall we be clothed? (For after all these things do the Gentiles seek:) for your heavenly Father knoweth that ye have need of all these things. But seek ye first the kingdom of God, and his righ-teousness; and all these things shall be added unto you. Take therefore no thought for the morrow: for the morrow shall take thought for the things of itself. Sufficient unto the day is the evil thereof.
(Matthew 6:25–34)

Our God is a God of provision. These verses clearly state that the Lord provides for our physical needs. Even more importantly, He supplies our spiritual needs, too. He takes care of *all* the needs that must be met in our lives. One of the most amazing provisions is His sending of the Holy Spirit, who is a Source of constant provision and comfort.

And I will pray the Father, and he shall give you another Comforter, that he may abide with you for ever; even the Spirit of truth; whom the world cannot receive, because it seeth him not, neither knoweth him: but ye know him; for he dwelleth with you, and shall be in you. I will not leave you comfortless: I will come to you. (John 14:16–18)

> *But my God shall supply all your need according to his riches in glory by Christ Jesus.* (Philippians 4:19)

Now Is the Time to Serve

God is tired of up-and-down saints. Do you remember what He said about lukewarm Christians? *"I know thy works, that thou art neither cold nor hot: I would thou wert cold or hot. So then because thou art lukewarm, and neither cold nor hot, I will spue thee out of my mouth"* (Revelation 3:15–16). If you have accepted Christ as your Savior, then you are His covenant child. He is committed to you; in response, He desires complete commitment from you.

God is tired of up-and-down saints; He desires complete commitment.

He doesn't want half-hearted commitment; He wants all of your heart. Think for a moment about the most important human relationship in your life. Maybe it's between you and your wife—or your husband, your best friend, your mom, or your dad. Whatever that relationship is, think about it for a moment. It sort of tugs on your heart, doesn't it? Maybe you feel a fondness for that person or a willingness to sacrifice things that are important to you for the sake of their well-being. When you're wholly committed to someone, your mind and emotions are involved. This is the kind of commitment God wants from you. Do you remember what He commanded the Israelites? *"And thou shalt love the LORD thy God with all thine heart, and with all thy soul, and with all thy might"* (Deuteronomy 6:5). He wants a commitment from you that requires your whole being.

Maybe you're reading this today and realizing that you've never made the initial one-time commitment that we discussed earlier. Have you accepted Jesus Christ as your personal Savior? If you have not done this, here is where you need to start. In accepting Christ as your Savior, you decide to commit the rest of your days to Him; in return, you become a covenant child, able to receive all the blessings He has promised for those in covenant with Him. If you have not accepted Christ as your Savior, I encourage you to do so. All it takes on your part is confession and belief: *"That if thou shalt confess with thy mouth the Lord Jesus, and shalt believe in thine heart that God hath raised him from the dead, thou shalt be saved"* (Romans 10:9). Do you believe? Are you ready to accept His gift and confess Him as your Savior?

If you've already accepted Christ as your personal Savior, I encourage you to seek after new heights of commitment. Are you ready to pursue the things of God, no matter how difficult it might be? Are you willing to keep your devotion to the Lord, even during the hard times? Are you prepared to love Him with your whole heart, soul, and might, even if it means letting go of other things that are important to you?

Now is the time to serve. The Lord is committed to providing for you. Why don't you commit to more fully serving Him? It is only then, when you are walking in His will as a committed covenant child, that you will be able to experience *"the breadth, and length, and depth, and height"* (Ephesians 3:18) of the Lord's love; it is only then that you can see His good and gracious promises unfold in your life.

Chapter Six

The Marriage Promise

Chapter 6
The Marriage Promise

One of the biggest commitments a person will make during his or her lifetime is that of marriage. Unfortunately, this is also one of the promises most often broken. Remember our statistic from earlier? Nearly fifty percent of all marriages end in divorce.

Why does this important commitment fall apart so frequently? Why are there so many couples retracting their marriage vows each year? I think a big part is an improper understanding of what marriage is. Until a person understands the solemn union that God intended marriage to be, that person will never be fully committed.

God intended for marriage to be an iron-clad promise. Look at how the Bible describes the first marriage, that of Adam and Eve. They were so committed that they became like *"one flesh,"* or one person, although they occupied two separate bodies.

And the rib, which the LORD God had taken from man, made he a woman, and brought her unto the man. And Adam said, This is now bone of my bones, and flesh of my flesh: she shall be called Woman, because she was taken out of Man. Therefore shall a man leave his father and his mother, and shall cleave unto his wife: and they shall be one flesh.
(Genesis 2:22–24)

This passage, along with many others from the New Testament, leaves no doubt that marriage is supposed to be a strong, solemn promise. Whether you are already married, planning to get married soon, or hoping to get married someday in the future, I encourage you to keep reading. When we clearly understand how God desires marriage to work, then we can pursue this intimate commitment confidently, joyfully, and worry-free.

The Paradigm: Christ and the Church

Anyone can run up to the altar and get married, but not everyone has the staying power to *commit* to marriage. Maybe you've heard people say things like, "If it doesn't work out, there's always divorce." This is the complete opposite of the biblical view of marriage. Scripture never refers to marriage as a "trial run," or something that can be easily abandoned as soon as it's no longer convenient.

Instead, the Bible compares marriage to the relationship between Christ and the church. Can you see Christ bailing out on the church? Can you see Him saying, "I'm tired of you, church. I think it's time for us to have a break. Let's get a divorce"? No way! Christ loves His church and is committed to it one hundred percent. A marriage should be the same. Let's take a look at the book of Ephesians for some specifics on how Christ's relationship with the church should serve as a model for marriage.

For the Ladies

Wives, submit yourselves unto your own husbands, as unto the Lord. For the husband is the head of the wife, even as Christ is the head of the church: and he is the saviour of the body. Therefore as the church is subject unto Christ, so let the wives be to their own husbands in every thing. (Ephesians 5:22–24)

The Lord wants women to give submission to their natural husbands just as they give submission to their spiritual Husband. *"Wives, submit yourselves unto your own husbands, as unto the Lord"* (v. 22). Now, there are two sides to this coin. First off, women are called to submit to their husbands and yield to their leadership. But the verse doesn't end there; it says *"submit yourselves unto your own husbands, as unto the Lord"* (emphasis added). In other words, husbands are to treat their wives with love, patience, gentleness, and grace, just as Christ deals with the church. Once a wife is being loved with the kind of love that Jesus gives, then it is easier for her to give wholehearted submission to her husband. When a husband starts treating his wife as Jesus treats her, then she'll more easily submit to him as she does to Jesus. We'll talk more about the husband's role in the next section.

I know it can be hard sometimes to submit because men can be such "knuckleheads." But this verse calls women to submit only *"unto your own husbands,"* not anyone else's husband. You don't have to worry about submitting to every man you meet; true submission is reserved for your husband alone, not for any other man.

A lot of people complain about this verse in the Bible, saying that it's sexist and things like that. But if you think about it, women desire to yield a certain amount of submission; this is how God has wired women to work. When a man takes a woman out on a date, for instance, the woman doesn't like to hear the question, "Well, what do you want to do? I don't have any ideas." She likes him to lead, to have a plan, to have things all figured out. This identifies him as a man with a plan. When she gets into the car and asks, "Where are we going?", she likes to hear him say, "You'll see." This assures her that she is special. If he hasn't taken time out to plan for their time together, she might feel ignored and unappreciated. But when he takes charge, she is satisfied and ready to submit to a man who so obviously loves her.

A woman likes a man with a plan.

For the Men

Husbands, love your wives, even as Christ also loved the church, and gave himself for it; that he might sanctify and cleanse it with the washing of water by the word, that he might present it to himself a glorious church, not having spot, or wrinkle, or any such thing; but that it should be holy and without blemish. So ought men to love their wives as their own bodies. He that loveth his wife loveth himself.
(Ephesians 5:25–28)

Okay, men, this part is for you. Your wife's submission is totally dependent upon the love you show her. As Paul said here in Ephesians, you are to *"love your wives, even as Christ also loved the church, and gave himself for it"* (v. 25). That is pure, self-sacrificing, and perfect love. Do you love your wife with Christlike love?

When you have Christlike love, you're willing to give anything for your wife, even your life. If a robber came into your house with a gun and said, "One of you must die," would you give your life? Or would you make some excuse like, "Take my wife because I have to support the family"? No, you must be willing to die. When a woman knows that you will die for her, she knows she's loved.

Think about all the things Christ had to dig through before He rescued us from sin. Think about all the maladies, the mess, and the miseries that surrounded us. And yet He still saved us! That is amazing love. He calls husbands to show the same kind of selfless love for their wives. If you had the same kind of love for your wife that God has for those He saves, then she'd be walking around like a peacock. When a man loves his wife just as Christ loves the church, submission is no longer an issue. It comes naturally as both spouses seek to glorify God and build each other up. And a woman whose husband really loves her has a radiance about her. You can see his love shining on her face.

The Two Become One

When you recite your wedding vows, you solemnly promise to love, respect, and honor your spouse, just as you naturally love, respect, and honor your own body.

> *For no man ever yet hated his own flesh; but nourisheth and cherisheth it, even as the Lord the church: for we are members of his body, of his flesh, and of his bones. For this cause shall a man leave his father and mother, and shall be joined unto his wife, and they two shall be one flesh. This is a great mystery: but I speak concerning Christ and the church. Nevertheless let every one of you in particular so love his wife even as himself; and the wife see that she reverence her husband.* (Ephesians 5:29–33)

As these verses from Ephesians show, there is a great union that takes place in marriage. In this union, Christ brings together two separate individuals until they become one person in the Lord. For such a union to work, the two must remain committed. They must really mean it when they say, "for better for worse, for richer for poorer, in sickness and in health, to love, cherish, and to obey, till death us do part." If they do not really mean it, the marriage is bound to crumble. Both husband and wife must rely on the Lord to help them fulfill their vows; otherwise, the *"one flesh"* will be torn into two.

Trust

Trust is essential for any relationship, especially when it comes to marriage. If spouses don't trust each other, they'll always be worrying and wondering what the other person is doing. This is no way to live a life of commitment. How can you be wholeheartedly committed to someone if you're always worried that that person is not staying committed to you? A relationship like this would be emotionally exhausting. For a marriage to stay healthy, trust is a must.

Why Women Don't Trust

Some women have a really hard time trusting because men have hurt them in past relationships. Upon first meeting a man, a woman might search for evidence that says, "He can't be trusted." The man may be completely trustworthy, honest, and concerned for her best interests, but because he is a man, she feels hesitant to trust.

In the body of Christ, however, there should be another level of integrity within relationships. There should be trust—both from the men and the women. We should not imitate the world's low standards for relationships; after all, the church is different from the world. *"Therefore if any man be in Christ, he is a new creature: old things are passed away; behold, all things are become new"* (2 Corinthians 5:17). According to this verse, we as Christians are new in our minds, our spirits, our orientations, and our ideas. We must make sure our relationships reflect the higher level of trust and love that goes along with this.

Men, I encourage you to help dispel the myth that men can't be trusted. Are you treating women with respect, honor, and the love of Christ? Or are you giving women good reasons for not trusting you? Move to that next level and prove yourselves trustworthy.

---

*If you had the same kind of love for your wife
that God has for those He saves,
then she'd be walking around
like a peacock.*

Women, I encourage you to let go of your fears and choose to trust men whenever they have proven themselves to be trustworthy. Is there a man in your life who has shown himself to be faithful and loving? Don't hold on to your fear of trusting when all the evidence around you says it's time to trust. Take a step of faith and choose to trust the man who has proven himself to be trustworthy.

When to Trust

How do you know if someone is trustworthy? How do you know when to take the leap of faith and start trusting? Trust isn't something to take lightly; before you give a person your trust, you need to know they deserve it.

The best way to tell if people are trustworthy is to look at how faithful they are to the Lord. Are they acting like the *"new creatures"* that 2 Corinthians 5:17 talks about? When you see that someone is truly committed to the Lord, then you know that you can fully trust that person. But if someone is not committed to the Lord, be careful about surrendering your trust. Why should you expect commitment from someone who won't even commit to the Lord? Why should you trust someone the Lord doesn't even trust?

During pre-marital counseling, I tell people all the time, "You know you can trust a man or a woman if you don't have sex together before you get married." Unfortunately, many people fail this test, but those who pass it pave the way for greater trust in the future.

You see, when you're in the body of Christ, your commitment first and foremost is to God. This commitment requires you to remain faithful to His laws, including His commandments against having sex outside of marriage. If you break this commandment, then how trustworthy are you? If you can't be faithful to God, then how are you going to be faithful to your spouse? Your faithfulness and commitment to the Lord is the best way for others to determine how faithful, committed, and trustworthy you will be in a relationship with them.

If you have sacrificed your commitment to God in return for sexual gratification, then you should stop, reevaluate your relationship with God, and repent. Now that you understand the sinfulness of your actions, you need only to say, "God, I repent. Please forgive me." You need to understand that if you have a sexual relationship with someone outside the umbrella of matrimony, then you're violating him or her and, more importantly, violating God's principles. That's why I continue to tell people, "Keep your commitment to each other pure. If you can discipline yourself before the marriage, then the probability of trust is greater for your future."

Do You Want to Trust or Not?

No one wants to come home to interrogation all the time. No one wants to hear, "Where have you been? I tried you on your pager *and* on your cell phone," immediately after opening the front door. This puts a person on the defensive.

A man who always returns home to questioning like this starts to prepare himself on the way home; he braces himself for the cross-examination and makes sure all his stories are straight, even if he's not guilty of anything. When he pulls in the driveway at 12:30 in the morning, he knows he has to face his wife's accusations, whether he's done anything wrong or not.

The tables can be turned, too; sometimes, it's the women who are on the defensive. A man might worry about what's happening at the water cooler where his wife works. He knows that she's attractive, and he starts wondering if other men might be making passes at her. Part of him wants to go to work with her and remind everyone there, "Hey, you know that's my wife," and another part of him wants to continually remind his wife, "He likes you, and I can tell, so stay away from him."

For a marriage to stay healthy, trust is a must.

I wouldn't want to live like this. If I had to worry all the time about trusting my wife, I'd rather live single. Unfortunately, many people choose to live like this.

If you're not married yet and are planning to be someday, make sure you get to know your future spouse really well before you race to the altar. It's important to know that you can trust the other person before you commit to a lifetime together. Examine his or her life. Is he faithful to Christ? Is she committed to keeping God's commandments? If you can answer, "yes," chances are good that that person is worthy of your trust. If you're dating someone right now, this should always be on your mind. If the person you're dating can't be trusted now, marriage isn't going to change a thing.

Some people think that there's going to be some mystical transformation after marriage, so that the man becomes a phenomenal husband and the woman turns into a super wife. No, what you see now is what you're going to get more of later. Make sure you like what you're getting into before you tie the knot.

If you are already married, work on building even stronger trust in your marriage. You can start by increasing your own trustworthiness. How? By making sure you are connected with the Lord. If you remain in the Vine, you're going to be fruitful, and your spouse will be able to taste that fruit through your increased faithfulness, love, and devotion. The biggest gift you can give your spouse is to make sure you're spiritually on track. When your relationship with the Lord is in line, a healthy relationship with your spouse will follow. *"But seek ye first the kingdom of God, and his righteousness; and all these things shall be added unto you"* (Matthew 6:33).

But what if you're on the other end? What if you're the one who's having trouble trusting? This is more difficult, because if your spouse is giving you reason to be suspicious, there's only so much you can do to change the situation. Since you can't determine your spouse's actions, you may feel hopeless. But even though you can't make decisions for your spouse, you *can* talk to your spouse about how you're feeling. If your spouse has given you reason not to trust, talk about it together. If your husband or wife desires an increased level of trust like you do, he or she will want to hear your feelings and will be open to suggestions for building that trust.

But before you sit your spouse down for a talk, make sure you have a real reason not to trust. Has your husband really done something wrong, or are you just looking for a fight? Is your wife really being unfaithful, or are you just having a hard time learning how to trust? Human beings can be stubborn creatures, and it's not unusual for us to hold on to feelings of jealousy, resentment, and doubt, even if the other person has done absolutely nothing wrong. Do you know what I'm talking about? Maybe you've done it yourself; your reason tells you that your spouse has done nothing wrong and is totally deserving of your trust, but the *"old things"* still inside of you won't let the *"new creature"* take over. (See 2 Corinthians 5:17.) Even though the "new you" wants to be trusting, the "old you" still wants to be guarded.

If I had to worry all the time about trusting my wife, I'd rather live single.

If this is the situation you find yourself in, work on developing your ability to trust. Remind yourself constantly of your spouse's faithfulness to the Lord, and remember that faithfulness to *you* arises out of this. When you develop a loving and trusting relationship with your spouse, you're going to stop riding emotional roller coasters all the time trying to figure out where he or she is. If I ever ask my wife where she is, it's not because I don't trust her—it's because I'm being just plain nosey. I don't go through these emotional ups and downs because there's a level of trust between us, as well as a history of faithfulness within our relationship.

When people do find your spouse attractive, don't get angry and defensive. Instead, thank God for the beautiful woman or the good-looking man He's given you. This reassures you of how special your spouse really is. Don't be upset, just thank God. Instead of throwing dirty looks, getting mad, and fighting over it in church, thank God for the special gift He has given you, and be assured that, although other people might look, your spouse is committed to you and you alone.

Respect

Just as trust is fundamental to marriage, so is respect. Without respect, a marriage will flop. Unfortunately, a lot of people don't realize this, and they settle for relationships where they get absolutely no respect whatsoever. I see this especially in the way some men treat women, and it's just not right. Ladies, if he wants your company, he's got to earn it by treating you with respect. If I were a woman, I would want the man in my life to open car doors for me and to not insist on going dutch every time we went out to eat. Ladies, recognize yourselves for the gifts that you are. You are women, and you deserve respect.

Disrespect can enter a relationship in other ways, too. I've seen some people, for instance, treat marriage as nothing more than a chance to have legal sex. "When I get married," they say, "I'm going to be able to have sex all day, and the Lord won't knock me for it." This is a sad reason to get married, and it shows complete disrespect. Real love respects the other person as a child of God and as a gift to be cherished—not as a toy to be played with. If you're planning to get married soon, I encourage you to take a close look at your relationship and make sure this form of disrespect hasn't crept in.

Problems of disrespect can arise after a couple is married, too, because familiarity often leads to complacency. In other words, the more I know you, the more liberties I take. Every couple is susceptible to this. When you first started dating, there were certain things you would never do for fear of embarrassing yourself. You wanted to impress the other person, and this required treating them with respect. But after a man and woman consummate a relationship, the mystique may be lost. When the honeymoon is over, respect may go down the drain.

An ideal marriage should work exactly opposite of this. If anything, respect for your spouse should flourish and grow over time. Since our natural tendency is to treat each other more and more casually with each passing year, we have to work hard at maintaining the mystique and keeping the respect. Yes, it does take work, but it's worth it. When you treat your spouse with respect, you strengthen your relationship and reclaim some of that lost mystique. But most importantly, you can know that you're being obedient to your Lord Jesus Christ by treating one of His children with the respect He commands.

So, the next time your husband does something you appreciate, tell him. Or the next time your wife goes an extra mile to help you out with something, let her know how much it means to you. Don't assume that your spouse can read your mind. Tell one another how much you cherish and treasure each other. This is the pathway to a marriage of ever-increasing intimacy and respect.

Endurance

Even with a strong foundation of trust and respect, your marriage is bound to face some hard times. Marriage isn't about pleasure only, just as your relationship with God isn't just about pleasure. Do you remember the serenity prayer? "Accepting hardship as the pathway to peace." Just as God uses spiritual struggles to strengthen our relationships with Himself, He also uses painful periods in our marriages to strengthen our bonds with our spouses. Yes, He has given you many good and wonderful things, but, oftentimes, those wonderful things arise out of painful situations that He allows you to experience. The development of the relationship between a husband and wife is not always pleasurable; at times it can even be painful. Some of the greatest conversations you'll ever have will arise out of adversity. To endure these hard times, you both need to be committed. Out of this will come fruit of faithfulness and trust—and the assurance that your marriage has been tried and proven true.

Chapter Seven

God's Abundance—Authority and Love

Chapter 7
God's Abundance—Authority and Love

As we've seen throughout this book, our God is a promise-making, promise-keeping God. Those who remain in the Vine have the privilege of tasting His sweet spiritual fruit, but those who do not abide in the Vine do not have this assurance. Remember, our God is a covenant-making God, and His promises of blessings are specifically for His covenant people.

If you've been a Christian for a while, you probably know that it's not always easy to remain in the Vine. Even though we know that's where we're meant to be, sometimes we still try to sever our connection to our Source of life. This is the continual struggle that every Christian must face until the Lord comes again to take us home. *"For the good that I would I do not: but the evil which I would not, that I do"* (Romans 7:19).

Whenever we face this struggle, there are a few key points to keep in mind. First, our God is a God of *authority*, and His will is that we would remain in Him; His authority is our primary reason for abiding in the Vine. Second, our God is a God of *love*; He is eager to forgive us, even when we do try to disconnect our lives from Him.

God of Authority

Our God is a God of authority. Whatever He says always comes to pass. We see this throughout Scripture, beginning at the very start, in Genesis, with God's act of creation.

> *And God said, Let there be light: and there was light....And God said, Let there be a firmament in the midst of the waters, and let it divide the waters from the waters....and it was so....And God said, Let the waters under the heaven be gathered together unto one place, and let the dry land appear: and it was so....And God said, Let the earth bring forth grass, the herb yielding seed, and the fruit tree yielding fruit after his kind, whose seed is in itself, upon the earth: and it was so....And God said, Let there be lights in the firmament of the heaven to divide the day from the night; and let them be for signs, and for seasons, and for days, and years: and let them be for lights in the firmament of the heaven to give light upon the earth: and it was so....And God said, Let the earth bring forth the living creature after his kind, cattle, and creeping thing, and beast of the earth after his kind: and it was so.*
> (Genesis 1:3, 6–7, 9, 11, 14–15, 24)

Did you notice the words that are repeated over and over in these verses? The phrase *"and God said"* is always followed by the phrase *"and it was so."* This reinforces the fact that whatever God commands *always* happens. He has authority like no other being.

Even God's name in the Old Testament reminds us that He is a God of authority. Do you remember what God told Moses when Moses asked God His name? God said simply,

"I Am That I Am" (Exodus 3:14). In going by that name, God reminded the people of Israel that He is self-existent and independent from any other creature. That was all He had to say. The fact that He merely existed was powerful enough. That is what you call true authority. God doesn't need anyone else to help Him see His plans through.

> *And Moses said unto God, Behold, when I come unto the children of Israel, and shall say unto them, The God of your fathers hath sent me unto you; and they shall say to me, What is his name? what shall I say unto them? And God said unto Moses, I Am That I Am: and he said, Thus shalt thou say unto the children of Israel, I Am hath sent me unto you.* (Exodus 3:13–14)

Scripture is packed with examples of the Son's authority, too, not just the Father's:

> *And they were all amazed, insomuch that they questioned among themselves, saying, What thing is this? what new doctrine is this? for **with authority commandeth he** even the unclean spirits, and they do obey him.* (Mark 1:27, emphasis added)

> *And a certain centurion's servant, who was dear unto him, was sick, and ready to die. And when he heard of Jesus, he sent unto him the elders of the Jews, beseeching him that he would come and heal his servant. And when they came to Jesus, they besought him instantly, saying, That he was worthy for whom he should do this: for he loveth our nation, and he hath built us a synagogue. Then Jesus went with them. And when he was now not far from the house, the centurion sent friends to him, saying unto him, Lord, trouble not thyself: for I am not worthy that thou shouldest enter under my roof: wherefore neither thought I myself worthy to come unto thee: **but say in a word, and my servant shall be healed**. For I also am a man*

> *set under authority, having under me soldiers, and I*
> *say unto one, Go, and he goeth; and to another, Come,*
> *and he cometh; and to my servant, Do this, and he*
> *doeth it.* (Luke 7:2–8, emphasis added)

It's very clear that our God has authority. He is Creator and Sustainer of all creation. He is self-existent and sovereign; all-powerful and all-knowing; immutable and ever-present. Our God is awesome and almighty, far beyond our comprehension. His greatness deserves our praise. *"Thou art worthy, O Lord, to receive glory and honour and power: for thou hast created all things, and for thy pleasure they are and were created"* (Revelation 4:11).

Notice the final words of this verse: *"Thou hast created all things, and for thy pleasure they are and were created."* In other words, God's very purpose for making us was for His own pleasure! Since this is why we were made, shouldn't we seek to give Him glory? If this is what He created us for, we won't be content doing any other thing. So, the next time you're tempted to sever your connection to the Vine, remember His authority. Remind yourself that He is a holy, perfect, and powerful God who desires, deserves, and, in fact, demands your praise.

Recognizing Whose You Are

When God created man, He created him in His own image, meaning God endowed man with some of His own characteristics and qualities. Mankind, for instance, is creative by nature; this creativity arises from God's creative nature. Mankind is capable of love, which springs from God's loving nature. And mankind has authority over the creatures of the earth, which flows from God's authority over *all* creation. It's almost like we have God's thumbprint on us; He has stamped little bits of Himself onto our souls, our spirits, our minds, and our emotions.

And God said, Let us make man in our image, after our likeness: and let them have dominion over the fish of the sea, and over the fowl of the air, and over the cattle, and over all the earth, and over every creeping thing that creepeth upon the earth. So God created man in his own image, in the image of God created he him; male and female created he them.
(Genesis 1:26–27)

Unfortunately, we've smudged God's thumbprint. When Adam and Eve sinned in the Garden, all the good qualities that God had given mankind became warped and distorted. Man could no longer love with pure love or be creative with God-honoring creativity; instead, all these good things became tinged with selfishness and pride. We stopped using these wonderful gifts for God's glory alone and started using them for our own advancement and pleasure.

God is a holy, perfect, and powerful God
who desires, deserves, and, in fact,
demands your praise.

Authority was one of those qualities that were damaged. Before they sinned, Adam and Eve had control over the creatures of the earth. *"Let them have dominion over the fish of the sea, and over the fowl of the air, and over the cattle, and over all the earth, and over every creeping thing that creepeth upon the earth."* They were stewards, or protectors, of God's creation. After the Fall, man was still assigned as steward, but his authority over earth's creatures was turned upside down.

And unto Adam he said, Because thou hast hearkened unto the voice of thy wife, and hast eaten of the tree, of which I commanded thee, saying, Thou shalt not eat of it: cursed is the ground for thy sake;

in sorrow shalt thou eat of it all the days of thy life; thorns also and thistles shall it bring forth to thee; and thou shalt eat the herb of the field; in the sweat of thy face shalt thou eat bread, till thou return unto the ground; for out of it wast thou taken: for dust thou art, and unto dust shalt thou return. (Genesis 3:17–19)

Once Adam and Eve sinned, they didn't have the authority they had once had. It was almost as if the plants of the earth were ruling Adam by making life so difficult. Unfortunately, the damage to man's ability to rule didn't stop here. I'm sure you know what I'm talking about. Think about it. Most wars, political disagreements, and even church disputes happen because of feuding about who's in charge. Before they sinned, Adam and Eve never had a problem glorifying God with the authority He had given them. They acknowledged God as the ultimate authority and recognized their authority as small and insignificant compared to His. But look at us now. Many go so far as to even question God's authority over their lives! Our understanding of authority has been warped.

Fortunately, God didn't leave us to sort through this mess on our own. Instead, He chose to redeem, or buy back, all the good things that mankind had damaged. He did this perfectly and completely in His Son, Jesus Christ. *"For the Son of man is come to seek and to save that which was lost"* (Luke 19:10). Jesus came to restore and renew all the things that we had messed up. In other words, when we accept Jesus into our lives, then our abilities to love, to be creative, to show authority, and to do all the things God created us to do are brought closer to how God originally created them. God does this through His Holy Spirit, who trains us in His ways.

But the Comforter, which is the Holy Ghost, whom the Father will send in my name, he shall teach you all things, and bring all things to your remembrance, whatsoever I have said unto you. (John 14:26)

Do you realize whose you are? I'm not talking about *who* you are but *whose* you are. You are a child of the King! You belong to Him! You don't have to be enslaved anymore by selfish desires, because He has restored your ability to use your gifts for His glory instead of your own. With His indwelling Holy Spirit, you can love, be creative, show authority, and so much more, knowing that you are doing it to bring praise to His name and not yours. This is a wonderful thing.

As a child of the King, you have other gifts from the Spirit, too. You have authority like you've never had before, simply because you're following the One who ultimately holds *all* authority. God wants you to know the authority that you walk in as a believer. Do you know your authority? You walk in the authority of possession—the authority to possess all the things God has promised to those who love Him. If you are a Christian, know that you possess so many things— peace, freedom from sin, access to the Father, eternal life, spiritual strength for the hardest of days, and joy like none other. As a child of the King, you have authority to possess all these things.

But be wary. The enemy often tries to distract us from our real authority by leading us on wild goose chases after our own power and possession. Satan knows that anybody walking in God's power understands what authority feels like, and he tries to deceive us into using our spiritual authority for selfish reasons. As a Christian, be prepared; you're bound to face temptations like this. The enemy hates God's power and will try anything to challenge it. If you are worth anything in the kingdom, you will face opposition.

Blessed are they which are persecuted for righteousness' sake: for theirs is the kingdom of heaven. Blessed are ye, when men shall revile you, and persecute you, and shall say all manner of evil against you falsely, for my sake. Rejoice, and be exceeding

glad: for great is your reward in heaven: for so per-
secuted they the prophets which were before you.
(Matthew 5:10–12)

So if you're going through what seems like a tremendous amount of endless opposition, it's because God has anointed and chosen you.

Sad Substitutions

Amazingly, even though we understand God's authority, sometimes we still try to replace Him. In our stubborn sinfulness, we think we know better than Him, and we let our selfish desires replace God's rightful position on the thrones of our hearts. In fact, this is what happens every time we sin.

Man cannot properly function
outside of God's glory.

As Christians, we often let God fall from the number one spot in our hearts. We have to remember that pursuit of earthly matters will never fulfill our spiritual needs. Boyfriends, girlfriends, or any human relationship will never fill the void, nor will alcohol, food, drugs, sex, or money. Only the presence of God can satisfy our hunger and thirst.

The reality is that man needs God. Man cannot properly function outside of His glory. Years ago, some of the people in the church I grew up in used to praise God with extreme emotional fervor, shouting praises like, "Thank You, Jesus!" and "Hallelujah!" Meanwhile, some of the mothers, who were the more seasoned worshippers in the church, would lift their hands and quietly say, "Glory to God!" You see, these women understood their need to experience the glory of God. *"Thou wilt show me the path of life: in thy presence is fulness of joy; at thy right hand there are pleasures for evermore"* (Psalm

16:11). They longed for His glorious presence, and they praised God for stooping to visit them. Even though they didn't show the emotional fervor of the younger worshippers, they did have a hunger for God's glory, and that's what mattered. This is what true worship is: realizing the glory of our God and praising Him for it. Nothing satisfies our souls like the presence of God's glory.

God of Love

No matter how deeply we understand the Lord's authority, we are bound to challenge it from time to time. Our goal is to live a life completely surrendered to God, a life that fully yields to His authority. Until Christ returns, however, there will be times when we do not surrender to God, times when we will question His authority. This struggle—a battle between the old creature and the new creature—is something that every Christian must face. Let's look again at Paul's discussion of this struggle in his letter to the Romans.

For we know that the law is spiritual: but I am carnal, sold under sin. For that which I do I allow not: for what I would, that do I not; but what I hate, that do I. If then I do that which I would not, I consent unto the law that it is good. Now then it is no more I that do it, but sin that dwelleth in me. For I know that in me (that is, in my flesh,) dwelleth no good thing: for to will is present with me; but how to perform that which is good I find not. For the good that I would I do not: but the evil which I would not, that I do. Now if I do that I would not, it is no more I that do it, but sin that dwelleth in me. I find then a law, that, when I would do good, evil is present with me. For I delight in the law of God after the inward man: but I see another law in my members, warring against the law of my mind, and bringing me into captivity to the law of sin which is in my members. O wretched man that I am! who shall deliver me from the body of this death? (Romans 7:14–24)

This is a little disheartening, isn't it? No matter how earnestly we seek surrender to our Lord or how passionately we pursue His holiness, we will still find ourselves falling short of the glory of God. Paul seemed to be discouraged, too, for he exclaimed, *"O wretched man that I am!"* Do you feel this way? Are you disappointed that, with all your efforts to live for God's glory, your heart still falls victim to sin? I admit, this can be downright frustrating for the Christian who wants to serve the Lord.

But you see, as long as we're living in the presence of sin, we're going to be affected by it. When we're saved, we're not suddenly transformed into perfect, sinless saints. Instead, God starts taking our lives through a process of progressive purification. Until our Lord returns and we see Him face to face, there will be times when we'll still struggle with sin.

Understanding the process of sanctification might make this clearer. You see, there are three levels of sanctification: instantaneous, progressive, and complete.

In instantaneous sanctification, God forgives our sins and starts seeing our lives through the shed blood of Christ. Instead of seeing all the sinfulness in our lives, God sees His perfect Son. *"For ye are all the children of God by faith in Christ Jesus. For as many of you as have been baptized into Christ have put on Christ"* (Galatians 3:26–27). As this verse suggests, it's almost like we're "wrapped up" in Jesus, or wearing His clothing.

The second level, progressive sanctification, is what you're experiencing right now if you're a Christian. Progressive, or maturing, sanctification is when God shapes and molds our lives into Christlikeness. God already sees His perfect Son whenever He looks at our lives because of instantaneous sanctification, but in progressive sanctification, God starts the process of making our lives actually resemble

Christ's. It's a long and often difficult process, and we'll be going through it until Christ's return.

Complete, or final, sanctification, is what we have to look forward to. In complete sanctification, our lives do resemble Christ's. It is only here, in complete sanctification, that we won't have to worry about the war going on inside of us, the war that Paul describes in Romans 7:21: *"I find then a law, that, when I would do good, evil is present with me."* But when Jesus Christ returns to get His people as described in 1 Thessalonians 4:16–17, we will be taken from the presence of sin. It is only then that our old sinful nature will be completely abolished. Complete sanctification isn't here yet; it's when He comes and completely separates us from sin. When this mortal shall put on immortality (1 Corinthians 15:53–54), we shall be changed. And we can certainly look forward to that.

> God is so perfect and yet so forgiving
> when we're not perfect.

Are you frustrated as you wait for complete sanctification? Are you annoyed that you still struggle with sin from time to time? This is the point where we need to remember that our God, a God of love, is patient and forgiving. And He never breaks a promise. He's the God of unbroken promises. Though we may break countless promises that we've made to God, His promises to us are still unbroken. He will never turn His back on us. *"I will never leave thee, nor forsake thee"* (Hebrews 13:5).

When you try to offer God your best, only to come up short, don't give up in frustration. Remember, *"for all have sinned, and come short of the glory of God"* (Romans 3:23). We could never earn or deserve all the good that God offers us. He is rich in mercy and abundant in grace, *"ready to forgive; and plenteous in mercy unto all them that call upon thee"* (Psalm 86:5). It is time for you to embrace a God of unbroken promises.

If our God of authority demands such high standards of service unto Him, how can that same God be so forgiving and loving when we fall short of His standards? This is one of the great mysteries, or paradoxes, of God's character: He is so perfect and yet so forgiving when we're not perfect.

Don't think that God can just ignore or brush over your sin. If it grieves you, then it grieves Him infinitely more. Whatever sadness you feel for the sins you've committed is no comparison to the sadness God feels. You see, our earthen vessels have a much higher tolerance to sin than God does. He cannot shrug off sin or simply ignore it as we sometimes do, for it angers and saddens Him deeply. Despite the pain He feels at seeing our sins, however, He still loves us deeply. *"But God commendeth his love toward us, in that, while we were yet sinners, Christ died for us"* (Romans 5:8). And because of the loving sacrifice of His Son, He can forgive our sins and welcome us back into fellowship with Himself.

There is therefore now no condemnation to them which are in Christ Jesus, who walk not after the flesh, but after the Spirit. For the law of the Spirit of life in Christ Jesus hath made me free from the law of sin and death. For what the law could not do, in that it was weak through the flesh, God sending his own Son in the likeness of sinful flesh, and for sin, condemned sin in the flesh: that the righteousness of the law might be fulfilled in us, who walk not after the flesh, but after the Spirit. For they that are after the flesh do mind the things of the flesh; but they that are after the Spirit the things of the

Spirit. For to be carnally minded is death; but to be spiritually minded is life and peace.
(Romans 8:1–6)

Once you become a Christian, nothing can separate you from God's love.

For I am persuaded, that neither death, nor life, nor angels, nor principalities, nor powers, nor things present, nor things to come, nor height, nor depth, nor any other creature, shall be able to separate us from the love of God, which is in Christ Jesus our Lord.
(Romans 8:38–39)

This is a promise from our God: *Nothing* can separate us from His love. When you fall into sin, don't dwell on it or worry that you've created a huge, irreparable chasm between yourself and the Lord. Instead, confess your sin to Him, repent of your sin, and remember your Lord's promise to always love you. Only then will you be ready to taste His mercy and His grace in your life.

God's Mercy

Often we lump the words *grace* and *mercy* together as if the two were interchangeable. They are not. Yes, they do go hand in hand, but they are two separate blessings from our heavenly Father.

Mercy happens when we don't get what we really deserve. Think of it this way: As sinners, we deserve a painful eternity, apart from Christ, in hell. *"For the wages of sin is death; but the gift of God is eternal life through Jesus Christ our Lord"* (Romans 6:23). We deserve the spiritual death that God warned Adam and Eve of in the garden. *"But of the tree of the knowledge of good and evil, thou shalt not eat of it: for in the day that thou eatest thereof thou shalt surely die"* (Genesis 2:17). What we really deserve is punishment, separation, death.

135

God in His mercy, however, provided a way for us to escape this eternal pain. He sent His Son, who bore our punishment for us so that we wouldn't have to. *"For as in Adam all die, even so in Christ shall all be made alive"* (1 Corinthians 15:22).

Mercy gives us access to the Son. Despite my guilt, God gave me mercy. Mercy says, "You're guilty, but I'm not going to treat you like you're guilty. You deserve punishment, but I'm not going to punish you. I'm going to treat you like my perfect Son."

So, this is mercy—the glorious gift of God that exempts us from the spiritual death that's rightfully ours.

God's Grace

We've already discussed mercy. It's defined as "not getting what we deserve." Grace has a different spin on it; it is getting what we do not deserve. In other words, God's grace is manifested in all the good and glorious spiritual gifts and blessings that He bestows on us, blessings that we really should have no access to. *"Blessed be the God and Father of our Lord Jesus Christ, who hath blessed us with all spiritual blessings in heavenly places in Christ"* (Ephesians 1:3).

Now, there's something you need to understand about mercy and grace. They are not one-time events. Some people think you ask for it once and that's enough. No way! We need to get on our knees every day and ask the Lord for His mercy and grace.

> *And he said to them all, If any man will come after me, let him deny himself, and take up his cross daily, and follow me. For whosoever will save his life shall lose it: but whosoever will lose his life for my sake, the same shall save it.* (Luke 9:23–24)

Even as Christians, we will still sin; but we must remember the mercy and grace that await us—the mercy and grace that allow us to abide in the Vine so that we may always taste and know God's unbroken promises. *"O taste and see that the Lord is good: blessed is the man that trusteth in him"* (Psalm 34:8).

About the Author

Mitchell G. Taylor

About the Author
Mitchell G. Taylor

Mitchell G. Taylor has served as senior pastor of Center of Hope International for over ten years. Center of Hope International, once known as Long Island City Gospel Church, is one of the fastest growing churches in Long Island City, New York. Mitchell began pastoring the church in 1991 at the request of his father, Bishop Moses Taylor.

Although raised as a "preacher's kid," Mitchell became acquainted with street life early on. He quickly got caught up in a life of drugs and crime. He spent several years in and out of prison and eventually developed an addiction to heroin.

God had other plans for Mitchell. After visiting his father's church one evening, he was supernaturally changed and gave his life to Christ. He has been seeking the Lord ever since.

Shortly after his conversion, he enrolled in the Bethel Bible Institute under Bishop Roderick Caesar, Sr., in Queens, New York where he completed classes in evangelism and general Bible. He continued his studies at the United Christian College in Brooklyn, New York where he earned his bachelor of theology degree under the instruction of Dr. Irene Powell. Mitchell also holds an Honorary Doctorate of Divinity from the United Theological Seminary in Orlando, Florida.

While still studying theology, Mitchell began his ministry with a tent crusade in 1983. Many souls came to the Lord during that meeting, and Mitchell has conducted several revivals since then, which the Lord has also used to change lives.

Mitchell founded his first church, Astoria Outreach Ministries in Queens, New York, in 1987. He pastored this church until taking over pastoring duties at his current church, Center of Hope Internationl.

Because of Mitchell's efforts in Long Island City, CBS News aired a national television special on him in April of 1994. The program, which refered to Pastor Taylor as "The Preacher in the Hood," spotlighted the outreach programs of Center of Hope International.

Mitchell has a love for gospel music, and he composes and arranges songs as the Lord leads him. For many years he served as the National Director of Promotions for Malaco/ Savoy Music Group, a vehicle for spreading the Gospel of Jesus Christ through song.

Pastor Taylor has been happily married to his wife, Barbara, for many years. They have two children, Telisha and Mitchell, Jr.

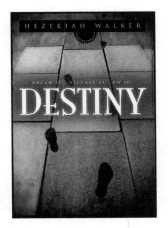

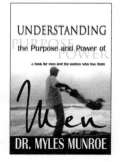
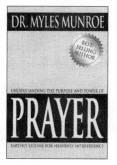